Thérèse Martin

Rosemary
Haughton

Thérèse Martin

THE STORY OF ST. THERESE OF LISIEUX

The Macmillan Company, New York

Nihil obstat: John A. Goodwine, J.C.D.
                   Censor Librorum
Imprimatur: ✠ Terence J. Cooke, D.D., V.G.
                   New York, April 8, 1967

ACKNOWLEDGMENTS

My thanks are due to the Carmel of Presteigne for a
great deal of help over details of Carmelite life, the
loan of books, and the typing of the original edition.
I am grateful also to a Dominican friend who read
and criticized the first edition and whose ideas helped
me to revise the book for the present one.

Photos from *The Photo Album of St. Thérèse of
Lisieux* © 1962 by P. J. Kenedy & Sons, used with permission.

CONTENTS

1. The New Baby

Just before midnight on January 2, 1873, Monsieur Martin went up the stairs and into the room where his two eldest daughters were sleeping. Gently, he wakened them to tell them the good news: "Children, you have a little sister." The two girls sat up in bed and with their father thanked God for the birth of the youngest in the family, the ninth child of Zélie and Louis Martin.

It was not until next morning that the two younger sisters heard the news, and later in the day all four visited their mother and the new baby. They crowded around the heavily draped cradle where the baby slept. Marie, the eldest, was thirteen, dark, a little stern sometimes, but with a quick wit—"my diamond," her father called her. Pauline, gentler, pretty, and intelligent, was eleven, and her nickname was "precious pearl." Next came Léonie, never very well, affectionate, but inclined to be jealous; she was the "odd one" in the family. At this time she was ten years old and, be-

cause of the naturally close friendship between the two
"big ones," turned for company to Céline, in spite of the
difference in age, for Céline was only three. There had been
other children. Hélène, a year younger than Léonie, died
when she was only four, and Léonie lost the one who might
have been her natural companion. Two years later a baby
brother was born, who lived only six months, and then
another the next year, who died as quickly. A year after
Céline came Mélanie, who died before she was two months
old. But the rest of the family still thought of these four
as alive and belonging to them. Later, they seemed to have
a share in the life of the youngest of all, who now lay, pale
and not yet very pretty, sleeping under the gaze of her
four sisters.

Two days later she was baptized in the church of Notre-
Dame in the country town of Alençon, in the northern part
of France called Normandy, and Marie was her godmother.
She was baptized Marie-Françoise-Thérèse, but she was always known by that last name. While the bells rang, Thérèse
was carried home through the snow-covered streets of Alençon to the house in the Rue St. Blaise where, above the
door, a marble plaque read: "Louis Martin. Fabricant de
Point d'Alençon," for this home was also the family's place
of business, where Monsieur Martin acted as agent for his
wife. It was her skilled work to assemble the pieces of the
famous *point d'Alençon* lace, made in their homes by workers
whom she had trained. Monsieur Martin had recently given
up his business as watchmaker in order to help his wife
with hers, and they were comfortably off, though by no
means rich. The house into which the maid, Louise, carried
Thérèse that day was comfortable and furnished with heavy,
ugly, but sturdy furniture. Upstairs, in her bed curtained
with thick plush, Madame Martin waited to see her newly
baptized daughter, and as she smiled up from her pillows at
her husband and held again the tiny shape of the baby in her

robe of white braided piqué, she prayed that this last child might stay with her and not too soon be snatched away. But she was a brave woman, and when the other babies had died she had told sympathetic friends that they should not cry for her. These babies were happy—and she had been allowed the privilege of caring for them during their short lives.

It seemed, a few days later, that her prayers for the baby had been unheard. Madame Martin tried to feed the baby herself and failed, for she was a tired and already ill woman. Thérèse got weaker, she was constantly sick, and the doctor said she would not live more than two days. She recovered for a few weeks, and then it began again. The only hope was a wet nurse, the doctor said, and Madame Martin remembered the woman who had nursed her two boys—she had not been able to feed them either—a farmer's wife called Rose Taillé.

Monsieur Martin was away, and after a night sitting beside the sick baby's cradle Madame Martin set off to walk to Semallé, about two miles away, where Rose lived. "Little Rose," they called her, because she was so small, but like many small women, she was very forceful and capable. But this time, she said, she could not come. What about the farm and her husband and all her own children? She was needed at home, she couldn't go—she was sorry, but she couldn't. Madame Martin, exhausted by worry and after a night awake, burst into tears and begged her to come, and Rose's kind heart was touched. She said she would come, but only for a week. Of course, her husband was furious, but Rose knew how to handle him, and in the end he gave in— until she and Madame Martin were out of sight. Then he sent one of their sons tearing after her to tell her to come back. But Rose was a determined person, and she had made up her mind to go to Alençon. She sent the boy home.

But when they reached the house, it seemed as if they were

too late. It was useless, Rose said, looking at the baby's pale little face with blue shadows around the eyes. Madame Martin dashed to her room to pray for the life of her baby, and when she came back Thérèse was already sucking strongly. But the sudden meal was too much for a baby in such a weak condition, and suddenly she became unconscious. She was so white and still that her mother thought she was dead and, numbed with sorrow, could only be thankful that she had died peacefully.

Thérèse was stronger than they thought, however, and after about ten minutes she opened her eyes and seemed to smile. She was getting better; and like most babies, once begun, she was soon quite well. After a week, Rose took the baby back with her to Semallé, since it was impossible for her to stay any longer in Alençon. Poor Madame Martin had to let her go, though it was hard to part with her baby. At Semallé, Thérèse fell ill again, but recovered—this time for good.

The farmhouse where Thérèse spent the next fourteen months had only two rooms, with a mud floor, stone walls, and a thatched roof. Outside the door were the yard and the stables, which were hardly ever cleaned; hens, goats, and pigs ran in and out of the room where the family lived. Thérèse throve on it. She grew, and grew fat—at four months she weighed fourteen pounds—and days out of doors made her brown and healthy. When she went out to the fields, Rose dumped the baby into a bed of hay in her wheelbarrow and took her along. At milking time she was fastened firmly to the back of the cow (Carrots was its name) while Rose got on with the milking. Rose's placid and kindly care was just what Thérèse needed, and she adored her new "mother," the only one she could remember.

When Rose went to Alençon, she took Thérèse with her and left the baby with her real mother while she did her marketing. But Thérèse was frightened, as babies of this

age are at being separated from their mothers, and she
screamed fiercely. One Sunday Rose left Thérèse with Madame Martin while she herself went to Mass, but the baby
screamed so hard that someone, perhaps a well-meaning
neighbor, sent a message to Rose asking her to come back.
Rose came hurrying back before Mass was half-finished,
and Madame Martin, who had been walking Thérèse up
and down in vain attempts to soothe her, was vexed. She
had not had nine babies for nothing and was unimpressed
by her daughter's furious yells. "She wouldn't have died of
screaming," she said a little tartly. But after that, when
Rose took her butter and cheese to market, Thérèse went,
too, and spent the day happily with the market women,
much petted and admired.

When she was fifteen months old, Thérèse left her beloved foster-mother, the country children who had played
with her, the fields and flowers and the animals, all the
world she knew, and came back to Alençon, to her real
mother and sisters. But they were strangers to her, and the
shock was severe. Gradually she became used to her home,
but she clung to her mother and refused to let her out of
her sight, terrified lest this second refuge should also be
taken away. Climbing the stairs, she stopped on each step
to call her: "Mother!"

"Yes, little one," her mother's voice answered, and
Thérèse, reassured for the moment, mounted another step.

In spite of her first fears of home, Thérèse soon showed
that she was really a gay and adventurous little girl. She
learned to use a tiny swing put up for her by her father.
She was so small that she had to be tied on, but she screamed
if it wasn't pushed hard enough. Her father certainly spoiled
her; she had everything she wanted, and he called her his
"little queen." Her sisters adored her, and the whole family
attended with admiration to every look and word of this
youngest and best loved of all.

She was an intelligent, lively child. She learned to say her prayers before she was two, chattered all day, and sang the tuneless little songs that toddlers often sing to themselves. She was taken to a part of Vespers on Sundays and watched everything with the greatest interest. If she couldn't go, she was furious and wept and stormed—there was nothing meek or gentle about Thérèse at the age of two.

2. The Little Queen

"MOTHER, I haven't said my prayers!"

"Go to sleep—you shall say them tomorrow."

"No, now!"

And Thérèse got her own way—she usually did. Her father came to help her say her prayers, but it was she who told him exactly what was to be said. "When she says 'no,' nothing can make her change," wrote her mother in a letter. "You could keep her down in the cellar all day without getting a 'yes' out of her. She would rather sleep there."

Adored by the whole family, showered with presents, dolls, and more dolls, with their clothes, tea sets, cooking stoves, why wasn't she thoroughly spoiled? Her mother watched carefully; she knew her obstinate, loving, willful little daughter. Though Thérèse was petted, absolute obedience was expected of her. When her father came home, she ran to him, sat on his foot, and was carried about like that, clasping his leg till she tired of it. Then he lifted her up and walked around the house with his "little queen" on his shoulder. Just the same, his will was law, and no slightest disobedience or impertinence was allowed to pass without reproof.

When she was two, she got into a rage over a game of bricks with Céline because she could not have her own way. Later on, when Léonie, grown too old for dolls, brought a basket of dolls' clothes and fascinating bits and pieces to Céline and Thérèse, telling them to choose what they liked, Céline chose a ball of pretty braid. Thérèse looked. Then, "I choose the whole lot!" she said and, seizing the basket, carried off her prize in triumph. She had a little vanity too. I should have looked much prettier with bare arms, she thought crossly, when her mother told Marie to dress her in a long-sleeved frock for a party. She had a violent temper if she could not have her own way, and even in bed she kicked all the bedclothes off and banged her head on the bedstead until her forehead came up in lumps.

"I have to punish the poor baby," her mother wrote. "She works herself up into frightful tantrums when things don't turn out as she wishes, and rolls about on the floor like a desperate woman who thinks all is lost! At times her temper is stronger than she is, it seems to suffocate her! She's a very nervy child." Thérèse was proud, too. When her mother laughingly offered her a half penny if she would kiss the ground, she refused to do anything so humiliating.

But with this fierce temper, obstinacy, and pride went great warmth of heart and generosity. From her parents she learned not only that they themselves loved her but that God loved her even more. Later, she remembered, "From the age of three I never refused God anything." She could never resist love.

She learned that Heaven was the home of God's love, so she wanted to go there. It seemed to her the only sensible thing to want. In order to get to Heaven, one had to please

God, one had to be obedient, to make sacrifices. Thérèse would do all this. "I will always behave like a little angel!" she told her mother confidently. And if she was bad and didn't get to Heaven, what then? Thérèse knew the answer: "I would fly up to you in Heaven, Mother, and you would hold me close in your arms. How could God take me away then?"

One day, when she was playing in the garden with her swing, her father passed by and called to her to come and give him a kiss. "Come yourself, Papa!" she answered. Marie, who was with her, spoke sharply to her. "You naughty little girl—how could you be so rude!" and straight away, Thérèse was tearing across the lawn, intent only on finding her father and being forgiven as quickly as possible.

In bed one morning, when her mother wanted to kiss her, she pretended to be still asleep. "She's only pretending," said Marie, but Thérèse pulled the bedclothes over her head, saying crossly, "I don't want anyone to look at me." Her mother left her and went downstairs. In two minutes, Madame Martin heard sobs, and there was Thérèse, tripping over her long nightgown in her hurry to reach her mother, tears pouring down her face. "Oh, Mama," she said, clasping her mother around the knees, "I *have* been naughty— forgive me!" She was forgiven at once, and afterward, as a special treat, her mother wrapped her in a blanket and cuddled her as if she were still a baby. It was always like that. She ran to ask forgiveness for every smallest fault or mistake, even quite accidental ones; she longed to make up for it, to put everything right. When she broke a little vase, she ran to show her mother, and seeing that she was upset, Thérèse was miserable. But a moment later, she came back. "Don't be sad, Mother. When I earn some money, I promise I'll buy you another!"

She loved her mother and father and her sisters, she hated to hurt them, and soon she began to love God in the same way. Her mother told her sometimes that little Jesus was not pleased at something she had done. She never wanted to do it again, for loving and being loved mattered more to her than her own wishes. So when she was taught that she could please Jesus by making small sacrifices for his sake, she set herself to offer as many as possible. Thérèse never did things by halves—neither her temper nor her sacrifices. Before she was four years old, she had taught herself to say nothing if anyone took away her toys. And if she was unfairly blamed for something, she kept quiet and did not make excuses. One Sunday she came back from an afternoon in the country with a large armful of flowers—cornflowers, daisies, and buttercups. She was beginning to arrange her treasure in bunches when her grandmother, who lived with them, came in and, seeing the flowers, said she would like them to decorate a shrine in honor of Mary, the Mother of Jesus. Thérèse watched her pick up the precious flowers and take them away; she said nothing to stop her, she did not complain, and if there were tears in her eyes, only Céline saw them.

Marie, her eldest sister, gave lessons now to Céline, and Thérèse, heartbroken at the idea of being separated from her playmate, pleaded to be allowed to sit and watch. They thought she would get tired of it, would fidget. But Thérèse sat for two hours without saying a word. She was given beads to thread or some sewing, and sometimes the needle slipped from her small fat fingers or came unthreaded. She sat there, her eyes full of tears, not saying a word for fear she should be sent away, until Marie noticed what was wrong and threaded the needle again.

They all adored her. Marie was charmed by her, and Thérèse admired her grown-up sister and obeyed her in everything. When, one day, her mother wanted to give her a rose out of the garden, Thérèse would not allow it. "Marie said I mustn't," she said. She was almost in tears, and when

Madame Martin cut two, in spite of her protests, nothing would make Thérèse have them. All the same, it was Pauline who had the greatest influence, which was odd because she was still a boarder at a school kept by nuns of the Order of the Visitation and seldom came home. Thérèse would often lean out of the window, looking toward the station. "What are you thinking about?" they asked her.

"About Pauline," she replied. She heard people saying that Pauline would be a nun. "I will be a nun, too," said Thérèse, aged two. Whatever Pauline did was surely the best possible thing to do.

"I'm going to be a nun in a cloister," she told Pauline one evening, when she was nearly four. "Céline wants to go, and after all, Pauline, people have got to be taught to read, haven't they? But I'm not going to teach, because it would bore me too much—that's for Céline. I shall be the Mother Superior. I shall walk up and down all day in the cloister, and then I shall go with Céline, and we'll play in the sand and with our dolls."

"My poor Thérèse, do you really think you'll be able to talk all day?" asked her sister. "Don't you know you'll have to keep quiet?"

"Really?" said Thérèse. "Oh, very well, then, I won't say a thing."

"What will you do, then?"

"That's not difficult—I shall pray to Jesus. But I don't know how I can pray without saying anything. And who will show me, do you think, because I shall be the Reverend Mother?" She considered this problem very seriously for some time, then she smiled and shrugged her shoulders. "After all, my little Paulinus, it's not worth worrying about yet. I'm too little, you see. When I'm big like you and Marie, before I go into the convent someone will tell me what to do, don't you think?"

"That's right," replied Pauline, loving her. "Now it's

late, time for bed, and I'm going to undress you. Wait a few nights before you call yourself 'Sister Marie-Aolysia' "—Thérèse couldn't pronounce "Aloysia" yet—"there's time to think it over."

It is more difficult to find out what she felt about Léonie. This third daughter, never really well and therefore rather backward in her work, was inclined to be moody and cross and seldom joined in the family conversations. She must have realized that the others disliked her behavior, however much they tried to hide it, and that made her worse than ever. But when the others went out for a walk, she could play with her baby sister, unwatched and uncriticized. Thérèse remembered later how Léonie sang lullabies to her and how the unhappiness and crossness disappeared when she talked to the youngest one, who was still too little to blame or misunderstand.

Thérèse's best friend and close companion was Céline, nearest in age, lively, sweet-natured, and docile. With her Thérèse discussed how to be good. She knew, though she could not have explained it, that "being good" means loving and that if you love you are willing to give up what you want for the sake of the person you love. So, for Thérèse, "being good" generally meant "making sacrifices." The little girls planned their sacrifices with great seriousness. They called them "practices." But there were a lot of other things to share besides "practices." Together they played with their dolls and with the bantam cock and hen which Louise, the maid, had given them. One morning, coming to dress the children, Louise found Thérèse's cot empty. Thérèse was in bed with Céline and did not want to get up. "Do leave me here, Louise. You see, we're like the two little white chickens—we can't be separated!"

On Sundays, while Thérèse was still too little to go to Mass, Céline was careful always to bring her back a little of the blessed bread which in France is sometimes distributed during Mass. (This *pain beni* is not the same as the consecrated Bread which people receive as holy communion.) Thérèse waited very quietly but, when she heard the door open, rushed out to get the bread, which she called "my Mass." One day Céline forgot it; it was a dreadful moment. But Thérèse had an idea. "You haven't any blessed bread? Well, then, you must make some!" Céline took some bread from the cupboard, recited a "Hail Mary" over it, and Thérèse, having made the sign of the cross, found it tasted just like the blessed bread from church.

Thérèse was growing up. She knew her alphabet, she could recite little poems, she was a "big girl." Her passionately loving nature turned more and more to God as the meaning and center of love, but very soon her understanding of God's love was to be tested by the death of the person she loved best on earth.

3. First Sorrow

B<small>Y THE</small> time Thérèse was four and a half, her mother was dying of cancer. Every morning Thérèse and Céline were fetched by a kind friend, at whose house they spent the day, so that they should not see how much their mother suffered. Perhaps Thérèse did not realize very clearly what it all meant, but she knew her mother was very ill, and both the children wanted to help as much as possible. The people who looked after them did all they could to keep them happy and amused, but it was no good. They gave Céline a ripe apricot. "We won't eat it," she whispered to Thérèse, "we'll give it to Mother."

But Madame Martin was too ill to eat apricots. The illness had first shown itself many years before, but for some reason nothing had been done. When the pain became too bad to be hidden any longer, her husband made her go to a doctor in Alençon, then to a specialist at Lisieux, a larger town some miles away from Alençon. It was too late; there was nothing the doctors could do at this stage. Madame Martin, who had just been told she was going to die of the disease, went home to Alençon and cheered up her family by telling them stories of people who had been ill with cancer and had got better. She carried on with her lacemaking, trying to finish all her orders. She did the housekeeping and looked after the children; she went to Mass every day. But she was getting steadily weaker, and the pain daily more severe, for the cancer was spreading. When her older daughters helped her to undress, they could see the red marks spreading to her shoulder.

In June, however, she went to Lourdes, the famous center of pilgrimage in honor of Mary. Marie, Pauline, and Léonie went with her to ask Our Lady to obtain her cure from God, as she had done so for many others, so that their mother might at least finish her children's education. The whole family set themselves to pray as they had never prayed before; they were sure they would be answered.

The pilgrimage was a nightmare. In the train the girls were sick, and some other travelers spilled their spirit stove all over the Martins' clothes and luggage. When they got there, the rooms that had been booked were filthy; they had to find others. The food was dreadful, the heat was exhausting. Madame Martin tripped on her dress in a crowd, fell, and twisted her neck, so that the pain was very much increased. Four times she was lowered into the icy water of the baths. This water has continued to flow since the day when the little peasant girl Bernadette was told in her vision of Mary, the Mother of Jesus, to "drink from the spring." There was no spring in the dank cave where the child saw her vision, but obediently she scratched at the soil and found it moist underneath. It was only some hours later that a trickle of water flowed from her muddy little hole, which has grown to a steady supply of thousands of gallons. Many sick people are bathed in the water at Lourdes, and some have been wonderfully cured, but Madame Martin was not among the fortunate ones. After the bathing, the pain was worse than ever, and she left for home, tired out by the journey and very much worse than when she set out. The girls could hardly believe that their prayers were unanswered and were silent and miserable. But Madame Martin was perfectly cheerful and managed to cheer up the rest of the family in the end. "Our Lady has said to me, as to Bernadette, 'I will make you happy, not in this world, but in the next,'" she told them. She came home and tried to carry on as before, but it was clear that she was much worse. She could not move without pain, and sleep was almost impossible.

Marie arranged one last treat for her dying mother, a last family feast. As she and Pauline had been at school at the Visitation convent, Marie called her little class—Céline and Thérèse—"The Visitation of St. Mary of Alençon," just as if their home were indeed a convent school, with a proper title of its own. She arranged a prizegiving for her "school" at the beginning of the summer holidays. She decorated her room with garlands of leaves and roses and dressed her pupils in white. Monsieur and Madame Martin sat in armchairs and gave out the books and wreaths to the two proud little girls dressed in white dresses and sashes with big white bows.

On August 26, 1877, Thérèse, kneeling near the bed, watched gravely while her mother received the Anointing of the Sick. The sick person is anointed with oil as a sign of healing, while everyone prays that the sick person may get better and be healed of his sins also. But at the time when Madame Martin died, it was the custom to give the Anointing only to people who were dying, or very nearly. After the Anointing, Madame Martin was given holy communion. When it is given to the dying, it is sometimes called "Viaticum," meaning supplies for a journey, for it is a preparation for the journey of death. Thérèse watched her mother's distorted face and heard sobbing all around her. She had been told that her mother was going to God. She could not realize what a complete separation this would be.

Two days later, Madame Martin died, a little after midnight. The younger children did not wake, but next day her father came to fetch Thérèse. "Come and kiss your mother for the last time," he said, and Thérèse, dry-eyed and silent, looked down from his arms at the face of her mother, serene and peaceful now after all the pain. She kissed the cold forehead.

Later in the day she came upon the coffin, which had just been brought in and was standing propped against the wall in the passage. Silently she looked at it, lifting her head to see its whole length, for she was very small.

Madame Martin's body was buried the following day in the cemetery of Notre-Dame. When the sad little group of her daughters in their black dresses came back to the empty home, they could only sit and look at each other. The maid, silly but well-meaning, wanted to show her sympathy for Céline and Thérèse. "You poor little things," she said, "you haven't a mother any more."

Céline, turning from her, flung herself into Marie's arms. "You will be our mother now!" she cried.

Thérèse would have done the same—she usually followed Céline's example—but the thought of Pauline's sorrow and loneliness stopped her. Slowly she went up to her favorite sister and leaned against her. "As for me, Pauline will be *my* mother."

When she was only a baby, Thérèse had lost her first "mother"—"little Rose" of Semallé. Now the person she loved best in the world, her real mother, had left her, too. Thérèse learned to think of her mother as still near her, watching over her. She was with God, who is love, and so the mother's love could not really be taken from her little daughter. But the shock of the loss was much greater than Thérèse, or any one else, realized. It was an experience that affected Thérèse's whole life.

4. The New Home

VERY soon after the death of Madame Martin, the whole family moved. Louis Martin did not want to leave Alençon. He had lived there so long, and all his memories were there, but he knew it would be better for the girls while they were growing up to have the help of their aunt, their mother's sister-in-law, who lived in Lisieux.

So they left the little house in the Rue St. Blaise, where Thérèse had been born and her mother had died, and arrived one autumn evening in Lisieux. Lisieux was not a little market town like Alençon, but a bigger and less attractive place. There was poverty there, such as Thérèse had never seen in Alençon, in ugly slum districts behind the smart streets of shops, churches, and the houses of the well-to-do.

Monsieur Guérin, their uncle—handsome, kindly, deep-voiced—met them at the station and took them to his home, where his wife longed to comfort the five motherless girls and their father. With her were her own two little girls, Marie and Jeanne, shy but friendly and full of interest. At this house they stayed the night and next morning set out to see their new home.

It was outside the main part of the town, on the hillside where many comfortable middle-class houses had been built, away from the smoke and noise of the town. The house was reached by a steep, stony little path. Suddenly, a door appeared in the high wall on one side, and there they were. It was a charming house, much bigger than the one at Alençon. When they came through the door from the road, they saw it framed in bushes and trees, a red-brick front with white stonework and window frames, rather like a doll's house. Right at the top, a little window set into the roof looked out over the treetops and over the whole town of Lisieux, which lay below them.

The elder sisters had little time to admire their home. The furniture was arriving and had to be unpacked, the house arranged and made spick-and-span. Their father had gone back to Alençon to settle some business but would come home in a few days, and there was a lot to be done.

Thérèse, left alone, set out to explore. She had been glad to leave Alençon, glad to get away from the sad house, from the awful memories of her mother's death, of the funeral, the sympathy of friends, the flowers, and the black crepe. She was not yet five, and the change was exciting: the train journey, the arrival in Lisieux, meeting her cousins—and now the new home. True, the house was still full of packing cases and shavings and piles of dusty dishes and bits of furniture in odd places, but there was the garden, and the garden was wonderful.

In front a small lawn was surrounded by bushes and trees which made a pleasant shade, and there were round flower beds near the house. At the back, the ground was higher, so that the lawn came up level with the first-floor windows.

Beyond the lawn were more trees and shrubbery and then a kitchen garden. There was a high wall all around the whole garden, and it was quiet and peaceful. Exploring every corner, Thérèse had forgotten for a moment that her darling mother was no longer there to share it with her. But the cheerful, mischievous Thérèse was gone. Since her mother's death, she had become timid, mouse-quiet, ready to cry at the least thing, terrified of strangers.

The furniture was arranged neatly. Monsieur Martin came home. What should they call the house? It had no name yet. They looked out of the window and saw the bushes surrounding the lawn, sheltering the house from the noise and bustle of the world outside. So they called it *Les Buissonnets*—"Little Bushes."

The routine of the household settled down. Thérèse and Céline had a room at the back of the house which looked out on the lawn. Here Pauline came every morning to wake Thérèse in her white-curtained bed, to give her a morning kiss and help her to say her prayers. They had onion soup for breakfast, cooked on an open fire on the red-brick hearth. Léonie and Céline went off to school at the big Benedictine abbey on the other side of the town, but Thérèse still had her lessons at home with Pauline and began the day with her reading lesson.

When her lessons were over, Thérèse rushed upstairs to her father's study—the big attic room whose windows looked out for miles over town and country—where Monsieur Martin spent long hours reading and praying. He had retired from his business now and could spend his time as he wished. He had never been an energetic man; he was naturally dreamy, retiring, a bit "odd." It had been his wife's strong character that had shaped their life together. Now, with enough money saved to keep the family comfortably, he was only interested in his daughters, his books, his prayers, and occasional expeditions for fishing. He visited his relations sometimes, but he lacked the vitality needed for much social life, and the Martins lived very quietly. He loved to be with his daughters, but most of all he loved Thérèse. The older girls accepted this as natural, and indeed they had a sort of veneration for their father, as if he had been something more than an ordinary human being. His aloofness and love of solitude impressed them as signs of holiness, and all his moods and wishes were accepted with complete obedience. Thérèse took it for granted that she was the favorite. It had always been so. Her father was never too aloof or too busy to talk to his "little queen," and she loved to show him her good marks when she had worked well and to tell him what she had learned.

Every afternoon, if she had done her lessons well, Thérèse went for a walk with her father. With them went the little white dog, Tom, and all three looked forward to it as the best part of the day. The walk always took them to one of the churches or chapels in the town. Thérèse and her father would spend a little while praying before the tabernacle—the cupboard in which, in Catholic churches, is kept some of the holy Bread consecrated at Mass, so that it can be taken to the sick and so that people may come to pray near this sign of Christ's presence among men. It was on one of these walks that Thérèse first saw the chapel of the Carmelite convent. Kneeling there, Monsieur Martin bent toward his little daughter and whispered, "Look, my little queen, there are holy nuns behind that big grille, always praying to God."

Tom did not particularly enjoy this part. He sat down on the steps outside, laid his head on his paws with a sigh, and waited patiently until they came out again. Then he would jump up joyfully and run ahead, leading the way to the park. On the way, Monsieur Martin talked to Thérèse about all sorts of things: about the poor and their needs, about France and her history. He taught her reverence by his example, baring his head whenever they passed a church or a Calvary, and he accorded the same gentle courtesy to all kinds of people. But he did not like too much exuberant talk or any frivolity. When people complimented him enthusiastically on Thérèse's prettiness, he discouraged them by a rather stern politeness. She loved to be allowed to carry the money her father gave to poor people. One day she was miserable because she thought she had offended an old cripple who politely refused her money. She cried and wished she could give him the cake her father had just bought for her, but was too shy to try a second time. Then she remembered that someone had told her that God would grant all one's prayers on one's first communion day. She cheered up at once; she would pray for the old man on that day. Five years later, she kept her promise.

When they got home, Thérèse finished her lessons and then went to play in the garden, digging in her own little garden patch or picking pieces of tree bark to mix with water in a pretty cup. This curious "tea" she took to her father, and he always pretended to drink it. Sometimes he asked jokingly whether he should throw it away, and Thérèse would snatch it back to use again later. She also made her own tiny cribs from twigs and scraps of stuff and arranged them in crevices in the garden wall. Her small fingers were as clever as those of her mother, the lacemaker.

In the evening they all sat round the big table in the living room. The girls worked at embroidery or sewing, Céline sometimes painted, and Thérèse sat on her father's lap and listened while Marie read aloud. Sometimes Monsieur Martin sang country songs, and later they went upstairs for prayers in the big girls' room, where stood the statue of Our Lady that they had brought from Alençon. Thérèse, kneeling beside her father, looked up into his face while he prayed, the face that looked so much older since his wife's death, and felt that she had only to watch him to see how the saints pray.

Pauline put her little sister to bed and kissed her good
night as she lay on her pillows under the pink silk canopy.

"Have I been good today? Do you think God is pleased
with me?" Thérèse asked anxiously.

"Yes," Pauline always answered and was glad that it was
a true answer, for if she had said "No," Thérèse would have
cried all night.

Sometimes the peaceful routine of the household was
changed for a family outing. In the summer they often went
out for picnics in the fields and woods outside the town.
The plates they used for picnics had funny pictures on them,
and they all enjoyed themselves a great deal. Thérèse loved
country walks: the green flowery hedges, where sometimes
she might see a nest with eggs or even little birds in it, the
fields deep in daisies, poppies, and cornflowers, the brooks
and shady trees. She was very happy when sometimes her
father took her out with him for a day's fishing. She sat
quietly on the bank among the tall grasses and watched
him and thought. Her thoughts were rather odd for a little
girl; the world seemed to her a sad place, far from home.
She dreamed of Heaven, and her thoughts became a kind
of wordless prayer. Sometimes she could hear the far-off
sound of a band in the town, and that made her feel a little
melancholy. She unwrapped the sandwiches on which Pauline
had spread such lovely red jam that morning, but now they
were soggy, the jam sunk in and pinkish. Thérèse was sure
that one could never find perfect happiness on earth.

Once there was a thunderstorm. Thérèse was thrilled and
sat watching the lightning and the huge raindrops like dia-
monds on the waving grass, until her father picked her up
and carried her back to the road and shelter. Thérèse almost
wished he hadn't, for she loved the rain.

One day in May the older girls had gone to the church
for one of the services which are held in Catholic churches
during this month, in honor of Mary, the Mother of Jesus.

Thérèse was too little to go, but she liked to have a "service" of her own, and she began to prepare the little "altar" on the chest of drawers in her own room, decorating it with flowers she had picked herself. Victoire, the maid, used to lend her bits of taper from the kitchen to fit her tiny candlesticks, and then they would pray together. That day, Thérèse asked Victoire to say a prayer to Mary called the *Memorare* while her tapers were alight, but Victoire only giggled. Thérèse, watching her precious tapers burn away, begged her to hurry. Victoire only laughed some more. With tears of rage in her eyes, Thérèse turned on her. "You wicked Victoire!" she shouted, stamping her foot. Poor Victoire stared at her, open-mouthed, and then showed her the two little pieces of real candle which she had been keeping under her apron as a surprise. Thérèse was bitterly ashamed and cried a long time in her remorse. She never forgot this incident, and it must have been much on her mind when, around this time, at about five, she was preparing for her first confession.

She talked about confession to Pauline, who taught her her religion as well as her ordinary lessons. "You aren't going to confess your sins to a man, my darling, but to God himself," Pauline told her.

Thérèse thought it over. "Since it is really God I am going to speak to," she said seriously, "should I tell Father Ducellier that I love him with all my heart?" Father Ducellier was a family friend, and Thérèse was fond of him, so when the time finally came for her confession, she walked sedately into the confessional and knelt down. But when Father Ducellier opened the shutter that separates the confessor's part of the confessional from the part where the penitent kneels, he could see nobody there. Thérèse was so small that her head had completely disappeared under the armrest, so she had to stand up. She was breathlessly still and attentive while she received absolution, remembering what an important moment it was. Afterward her rosary was blessed, and she left the confessional, very happy. On the way home through the darkening streets, she stopped under a lamp, pulled out the newly blessed beads, and began looking them over carefully.

"What are you doing, Thérèse?" asked Pauline.

"Trying to see what a blessed rosary looks like," replied Thérèse, and Pauline, very much amused, was impatient to get home and repeat the joke to the others.

Thérèse went to confession before all the big feast days of the Church. Every time she went, it seemed to her that she was sharing something of the happiness of Heaven. The love of Christ that opened her own heart to love was the thing that made her hate even the smallest fault, for faults were barriers that shut out love.

But Thérèse wasn't always as penitent as other people seemed to expect. On one occasion Victoire couldn't be bothered to reach down an inkpot from a high shelf, though Thérèse asked her ("quite politely," she remembered). Victoire only told Thérèse to get a chair. She got the chair, but she wasn't prepared to leave it at that, and she searched for the rudest words she knew with which to tell Victoire what she thought of her. Victoire herself had sometimes called Thérèse a "little brat," so now, standing on the chair, she turned to the maid and said, with immense dignity, "Victoire, you're a brat!" Then she jumped down and ran for shelter, but later she was made to apologize. She wasn't really sorry, though. If Victoire was so disobliging, what else could one call her?

But another time it was Victoire who rescued her from an ignominious position. She had been, as usual, balancing on a chair, when she slipped and fell seat first into a pail of water that Victoire had put down. With her feet touching her head, Thérèse remained stuck fast, while Victoire gaped at her frantic struggles to get out. She couldn't move, but finally Victoire pulled her out; and she had to change all her clothes, for she was soaked "like a piece of bread in the soup."

Another time it was the ashes of the fireplace that had to be brushed off her clothes. Thérèse was never still, always exploring, experimenting, learning. The placid routine at *Les Buissonnets* was only the framework for Thérèse's adventures.

5. Great Days

THERESE made her own games and private adventures
at home, but there were other breaks in the daily
round, among them the great feast days. These were
treats long expected and long remembered. The meaning
of each feast was carefully explained by Pauline beforehand,
and Thérèse felt she understood perfectly. Best of all she
loved the Corpus Christi processions, and when she was old
enough she was allowed to join in. The procession started
from the cathedral, and the brilliant colors of the priests'
vestments appeared first from under the gray arch of the
porch, then the choirboys and acolytes followed with their
silver censers and beautiful banners, embroidered in gold
and bright colors with pictures of Our Lady and the saints,
the patrons of different parishes and societies. In the center of
the procession a priest carried a gold monstrance, a round
frame inside which could be seen the host—the consecrated
Bread of the Eucharist. In front of the host went a crowd

of little girls dressed in white and crowned with flowers, their baskets full of rose petals to scatter before the priest who bore the Sacrament of the Body of Christ. Among these little girls was Thérèse. Her white piqué dress had pleats around the hem and was decorated with bands of heavy lace; it had a huge sash of fine pink silk, matching her wreath of pink roses. She was so happy, she wanted to sing as she threw up her petals, hoping that perhaps some would touch the host in the great gold monstrance. After the host came girls and boys who had made their first communion, wearing their white dresses or armbands; then there were the Children of Mary, a group of women and girls who called themselves after the Mother of Jesus and took her as their model. They were dressed in white and blue. Next came groups of nuns and religious orders of men and all the various societies and organizations of the parish, and after them followed all the rest of the congregation. Along the road were hung draperies of white cloth scattered with flowers. Little altars, or "resting-places," at the roadside were covered with flowers, too, for there the procession would pause while the host was raised in blessing over the kneeling crowds. In centuries when many Catholics had lost sight of the meaning of the Eucharist as a meal "which we share," few people received holy communion more than once a year. But they still wanted to show their devotion to Christ, and these gorgeous and gay processions were a way of doing this that everyone enjoyed. So they were and are a traditional part of Catholic life.

Christmas at *Les Buissonnets* was a great occasion. Days before, Monsieur Martin chose the great log which would burn in the open fireplace, and Thérèse anxiously supervised his choice and watched him bring it in. On the brick hearth were placed the children's shoes for the Holy Child to fill with presents. In France it is not Santa Claus who is expected to fill the children's stocking, but the Holy

Child himself who fills French children's shoes with presents. They are unwrapped when the family comes back from midnight Mass. So while the blazing log crackled and sparked, the little girls opened one wonderful parcel after another, squeaking with delight and surprise. Then there was the Christmas crib to admire, the big grand one in the church as well as the little one at home, and, in the evening, nuts and apples to roast on the fire, and stories to listen to, the old Christmas legends from Brittany that Monsieur Martin told so well.

The big feasts were far apart, but every week brought its own feast day that Thérèse loved dearly. This was Sunday. On Sundays, Thérèse was allowed to stay longer in bed than usual, and Pauline brought her a cup of hot chocolate before she helped her little sister to dress in her best dress, "like a princess." Marie brushed her long hair for her (Thérèse didn't like this), and then the whole family went to High Mass. As their usual places were in a side chapel, where they could not hear very well, they moved to places nearer to the pulpit when it was time for the sermon. The church was always packed, but everyone was ready to make room for the Martins. Often the sermon was too difficult for her to understand, but then she could watch her father's face, which told her so much, as he listened, about the love of God and the longing for Heaven. If the preacher mentioned St. Teresa, Monsieur Martin would bend down and whisper, "Listen, little queen, he is talking about your patron saint," and Thérèse would sit up, all attention. But the first sermon she really understood was when she was five and a half. It was about the Passion, the sufferings of Christ. She understood that Christ suffered all this out of love, and the idea made a deep and permanent impression on her.

But Sundays had to end, and after Compline, Thérèse was no longer so gay. Tomorrow was Monday—lessons, or-

dinary daily life again. Only in Heaven would it be always
Sunday.

Sometimes Sunday evening ended more happily for Thérèse. The girls took turns every week visiting their Uncle
and Aunt Guérin, and Thérèse enjoyed these visits very
much. She loved her kind, motherly aunt, and she liked to
listen to her uncle talking about all sorts of grown-up things.
He used to take her on his knee and sing a song called "Blue
Beard" in his deep rumbling voice. He wanted to amuse
her, but she was sometimes a little frightened. At eight
o'clock, her father came to fetch her, and they walked home
through the dark streets together. She liked to watch the
stars. Up there was the group called Orion, whose belt and
sword make the letter "T" in the sky, and Thérèse, delighted, clutched her father's hand.

"Look, Father!" she cried. "My name's written in Heav-
en." It was so exciting, she wanted to go on and on looking,
so her father led her home while she walked with her face
lifted to the stars.

There were family feast days too. One was the yearly
prizegiving. Although Thérèse was the only pupil whom
Pauline now taught, she never got a prize unless she had
earned it. Pauline wanted good work from her, and she got
it. First her report was read out before the whole family,
and then she went up to her father to take her prizes.
Thérèse thought it was rather like the Day of Judgment.
Afterward the girls very often did a play for the friends and
relations who were there.

Then there were the days of their special saints. Thérèse
loved best St. Céline's day, on October 21, and was very
scornful of calendars that left out that feast, for Céline was
her best friend. It was with Céline she had competitions in
arranging flowers or played at "schools" with all their dolls.
So when Céline's day came around, she was allowed a few *sous*
to buy presents for her sister, and she was determined to get

at least five or six different ones. Céline did the same for her on the feast of St. Teresa of Avila, on October 15, and both of them bought things for New Year's Day. They had not much pocket money, but when their father took them to a big department store to do their shopping, they would separate and hunt for the prettiest things they could find for their money. It was fun to see who had managed best.

When Thérèse was six, something happened to her that she remembered vividly all her life. Later on she wrote it all down, so we know exactly what happened.

Monsieur Martin was away from home and not expected back until late. About two o'clock in the afternoon, Thérèse was standing at a window looking over the back garden, thinking of pleasant things and enjoying the sight of the smooth lawn in the sun, with the trees beyond. Then, across the garden by the washhouse, she saw a man dressed exactly like her father, of the same height and with the same way of walking, only much older and with a stoop. At least she got the impression that he was older, but she could not see his face; it was heavily veiled. Slowly, steadily, he came toward her, passing her own little patch of garden. Suddenly, she began to feel frightened. "Father! Father!" she cried, her voice trembling. He did not seem to hear, did not even turn around, but went straight on to where a group of fir trees divided the main path of the garden. She waited, expecting him to come out on the other side of the trees, but nothing happened. He was gone.

Marie and Pauline heard her call, and frightened by her tone, they came running to see what was the matter. Controlling herself, Marie asked quietly, "Why are you calling Father like that, when he is in Alençon?"

Thérèse told her what she had seen, and Pauline tried to comfort her. "It must have been Victoire putting her apron over her head to try and scare you," she said. But Victoire swore she had never left the kitchen. Besides,

Thérèse knew quite well she had seen a man, a man just like her father. They went out and looked behind the clump of trees, but there was nothing there.

"Don't think about it any more," said Pauline. But Thérèse could not forget. Over and over again she puzzled about it, wondering what it might mean, and many years later she understood. Meanwhile, her father came home, perfectly well, and in her relief Thérèse let the frightening vision slip to the back of her mind.

She loved her father very dearly, and the idea that harm might come to him was too dreadful to be thought of. She admired everything he did and said and loved to listen to him when he talked about history or politics. "If you talked like that to the great men in the government," she said, "they'd be sure to make you king, and then France would be happier than ever before. The trouble is you would be miserable—kings always are—and also you wouldn't be my own special king, so I'm glad they don't know you."

It wasn't just what he said that she noticed and remembered, but the way he lived. Every day he was up in time to hear Mass at six o'clock, even if it was raining or snowing, and Marie and Pauline went with him. He liked the early Mass best, because all the poor people were there, God's favorite children. He gave away more and more money, but his idea of helping the poor was not just to give money. He gave himself. He visited people in need and helped them personally, sometimes he brought them home. Often, when he had been working in the slums, he came back in such a dirty state that he would not allow his daughters to touch him until he had washed and changed all his clothes. Louis Martin was not a naturally active person, but when someone needed him, he overcame his shyness and lethargy. His daughters learned to be as generous as he was, and as careless of their own comfort, but Thérèse was at this time still too little to be allowed to help.

The Martins did not spend all their time in Lisieux. They went for holidays sometimes, and it was when Thérèse was about seven that she first saw the sea. The Guérin family often went to Trouville for a holiday in the summer, and this time Thérèse and her father and sisters went with them. When she caught her first glimpse of the sea, she just stood and looked and looked. It was so huge. The roaring of the waves, their relentless power, made her think deeply about God, who was their creator. She was used to hearing people talk in a rather cozy and overly sweet way about God. The sea gave her another notion of him—it was vast and uncontrollable and majestic.

The children had great fun. They went shrimping, they rode on donkeys. Thérèse and her father went for walks along the promenade, talking and looking over the parapet at the changing colors of the water, and it was not surprising that people noticed the tall, handsome man with his white hair and the child who looked like a princess in a fairy tale.

"What a pretty little girl! Is she yours?" asked a lady passing by with her husband. Monsieur Martin was pleased, but he showed clearly enough that he didn't want his daughter praised to her face. He need not have worried. Thérèse was a sensible person and knew that if she was pretty it was not her doing, so it would be very silly to be conceited about it. But it was nice to know that she was pretty. She hadn't thought so before.

That same evening, Thérèse went with Pauline to watch the sunset from a lonely rock above the bay. They sat together and saw the sun make a shining path across the water as it went down. Thérèse remembered a story she had read called "The Golden Track," and it seemed to her that the shining path across the sea was a kind of sign. She thought that she herself was like a ship, and she resolved to steer her ship along the path of the light which is Christ so that she would come safely to harbor. She liked to think in pictures like this; they helped her to understand her life and her feelings. And she often shared her ideas with Pauline, who really did try to be a second mother to her little sister. Pauline could still teach her a great deal about her religion. But in other subjects, Thérèse was getting too big for Pauline's lessons at home. It was time she went to school. So when Léonie, who was nearly grown up, left the Benedictine abbey school, Thérèse took her place there as a day girl with Céline.

6. *The Schoolgirl*

"So Therese has no conscience!" the class mistress said sharply. Thérèse burst into tears. She was always bursting into tears. This time she had prompted another girl who had forgotten an answer, and it was more than two weeks before she could be comforted. "I have sinned, and I have made someone else sin!" she repeated. Naturally the other girls thought her very silly and teased her unmercifully.

Now that she was no longer at home, the dreadful shyness that had come over her at her mother's death showed itself much more. While she was with people she knew and loved, she was happy and gay, though always a quiet little girl. At school it was different.

The Martin girls walked to school with Marie and Jeanne Guérin, meeting them at their father's shop. All the children were taken and left at the big school door by the Guérins' maid, and as she saw the gray walls of the abbey

ahead, Thérèse's heart sank. She hated the muddle and noise
of the cloakroom. There she took off her coat and appeared
in her black serge uniform-dress with a short cape and a little
white bonnet, and while all the other girls gathered in chatter-
ing groups, Thérèse, once separated from Céline, was alone.

She liked learning things and worked hard, so she did
very well at her lessons. The first class she was in was called
the "green" one because the girls in it wore green belts on
their dresses, but although two years was the usual time to
spend in each class, Thérèse was moved up at the end of a
year into the "purple" class. In the green class she had been
one of the youngest, in the purple class she was far younger
than the rest. In spite of this she usually was first in everything except mathematics and handwriting. The nuns were
very pleased with her, and her father was delighted, but it
is not surprising that the other girls in the class were annoyed. They thought her weak and silly, they teased her
and bullied her, and because she didn't answer back, they
decided she was a coward as well. Besides, she was bad at
games. She wasn't used to outdoor games with other children, and when she tried to join in, she did it clumsily. She
soon decided it was no fun to play, when she did it so badly,
and kept away. Her extreme shyness prevented her from
making the effort to become better at sports. That was one
more bad mark against her. There was one girl in particular,
fourteen years old and rather stupid, who never lost a chance
of teasing and tormenting her. Thérèse longed for friends,
wanted to join in, to be liked, but the others soon made it
clear they did not want her, and her dreadfully easy tears
flowed constantly. She could not help it—no one realized
what was the matter with her, and even the kind nuns were
irritated by her crying and thought her uninteresting, though
a good little girl.

Every day she had that awful sick feeling at the sight of
the big school door, every day she found some comfort in

her work, and every day she hated the time for break or playing outside. In the playground, she kept away from the girls of her own class. Sometimes she could talk to Céline, often she would walk around with a book, trying to forget the outside world. Sometimes she carefully buried a dead bird she found in a corner of the playground—a melancholy game that suited her self-pitying mood.

The girls had midday dinner in a long, high room with tall windows where the day girls sat at the middle table. Each child brought her own set of knife, fork, spoon, and cup, and Thérèse's was a lovely set, the cup a silver goblet and the spoon and fork heavily chased. Perhaps in that bleak room it was a comfort to have something from home. They had plain food—boiled beef, soup, or stew; good, but usually lukewarm by the time the lay Sister had brought it from the faraway kitchen to the refectory. While they ate, one of the nuns read aloud from the lives of the saints and martyrs, including all the details of their sufferings. It did not help the girls' appetites, and the more imaginative ones sometimes couldn't help crying into their plates. Twice a week there was baking at the convent, and then there were hot, crisp cookies or apple cake for tea.

During the long dinner break, Thérèse often slipped away from the playground into the nuns' choir of the chapel, as all the girls were allowed to do if they wished. As she went in, the noise and chatter died away behind her, the peace of the quiet chapel seemed to soak into her, the irritations and sufferings of her school life dropped from her and were forgotten for a while. She was alone with the one person who would never let her down, never fail to understand, never turn away from her. Kneeling quietly in her place, she knew he was there, her Lord and her friend, and she loved him with her whole heart. There was no need of words between them—they knew each other too well.

So she endured the long classes, the teasing and cattiness.

She was very sensitive, and these things hurt her, but no one knew. She did not complain, she never talked about them, even to her father. Unhappy children often keep their miseries to themselves, though they could not tell why. Thérèse accepted her unhappiness as simply part of life. It did not occur to her that it could be changed, but by accepting it and by trying in spite of it to be reasonably cheerful at home for her father's sake, she learned some self-discipline.

As time went on it became easier. There were things she learned to love at school: the old, peaceful buildings; the traditions of the great abbesses, noble ladies many of them, who had shaped the history of the abbey; the kindness of some of the nuns, particularly Mother Sainte Placide, the Headmistress, whom she grew to love dearly. This nun came from a great family, but her mother had become a nun a few years after her husband's death, and with her went their beautiful daughter, who was then fifteen years old. They took the habit on the same day.

Mother Sainte Placide noticed Thérèse. She saw how she was treated and how she took it. She saw her at prayer, she watched her in class. She noticed how careful she was in keeping the rules, how glowing was her smile, and how gentle her manners.

But though Thérèse was not happy at school, she was not always there. For one thing, there were Thursday's half-holidays. Sometimes Thérèse played with her cousin Marie in the Guérins' garden, but she didn't like it when they spent the afternoon in dancing, which bored her. Sometimes they went to the park, where they played at being hermits, taking turns digging the garden and praying.

One day on the way home from school, Thérèse wanted to carry on the hermit game by meditating as they walked along. "You lead me," she said to Marie. "I'm going to shut my eyes."

"But I want to shut mine too!" said Marie, and they both did.

They were walking on the pavements, and it was all right for a bit, but they did not see the crates of vegetables which a greengrocer had stacked outside his shop. They walked slap into them, sending the lettuces and onions flying into the gutter. The greengrocer, not surprisingly, was furious, and the two hermits, with eyes very wide open, raced for home as fast as their legs would take them, while Jeanne came scolding behind them.

They did not try that again, but the Thursday games continued, and, of course, Thérèse had her beloved Sundays. Besides, there were the holidays at the seaside in the summer, when the girls took turns going to stay with the Guérins, who always took a house there for the holidays, usually at Trouville or Deauville.

But meanwhile something happened which caused far more pain to Thérèse than her unhappy days at school. When she was a very little girl, she and Pauline had talked about the fathers of the desert, who had left their homes to spend their lives in prayer in lonely places. Half in fun, Pauline once promised that if she wanted to go into the desert, she would wait until Thérèse was old enough to come too. But that was a long time ago. One evening, when Thérèse was nine, she was doing her homework while Marie and Pauline talked at the other end of the room, speaking softly so as not to disturb her.

"I've seen the Prioress of Carmel," she heard Pauline say. "I shall probably enter next month."

Thérèse was appalled. Pauline, her "little mother," her friend and teacher and adviser, the sister who comforted her for her unhappiness at school, was going away, leaving her. She had promised to wait, and yet she was going. Thérèse was old enough now to think about her own feelings, and even as she sat there, crying painfully, she was telling herself that she must realize how life is bound to be full of pain and separations. But for all her attempts at fortitude, the shock was worse even than that of her mother's death.

Once more, her security was being snatched from her. Deep inside her, something struggled desperately against a threat to her whole being, and it came to the surface of her mind as a wordless cry of despair. How could Pauline, who said she loved her, do such a thing to her?

Pauline was good and kind, but she had little understanding of a child's mind or of the lasting damage that she was doing to her sister. She felt that if only Thérèse understood, she would not mind so much and would learn to accept the separation with a goodwill. Gently, she drew Thérèse to her side and explained. Nowadays, she said, it was not easy to find real deserts into which to go, but people who wanted to give their lives to God in solitude could go into enclosed convents, where there was nothing to distract them from the service of God, where the noisy world could not enter. That was what Carmel was, and that was why Pauline was going there. And, she added, when Thérèse was older, she could follow her.

Thérèse listened quietly to all she had to say, then she went away and thought about it. The more she thought about it, the more beautiful the Carmelite life seemed to her. To live for God alone, to give up for his sake all other comfort, to be his in a specially close and intimate way—these were the things which she had wanted ever since she could remember, and here at last was the way to get them. It would be a hard life, she knew. One had to be very sure that such a life was what God really wanted. But Pauline had been sure. Suddenly a light seemed to go on in Thérèse's soul, showing her that Carmel was her place, too, the desert in which she could hide. From that moment on, she was quite certain of her vocation. She did not realize that, at this stage of her life, she seized on that idea of a Carmelite life so strongly just because Carmel was somewhere to hide. Later, Carmel became for her anything but an escape from living, but at nine years old Thérèse really needed to feel that she could find a refuge, a safe hiding place. She was loving and strong underneath, but too many shocks had battered at her sensitive mind before she was old enough to deal with them. All she could do was retire into herself, become shy and silent, and dream of a place where she would be safe from the brutalities of the world. Her love of God was sincere and generous, but it had to overcome a great deal of fear before she could grow up to love freely and bravely.

The next day she told Pauline what she had decided. Pauline never doubted that Thérèse was right, that although she was only nine, this call was from God. She arranged to take her to see the Prioress of Carmel, Mother Marie Gonzaga, and Thérèse told her about her vocation as well. Mother Marie was kind to her and said she thought she had a vocation. "But," she added, "we don't take postulants who are only nine. You will have to wait until you are sixteen."

So Thérèse went home, and life went on as before. She plodded through her lessons, endured the hours of recreation in the playground. Sometimes she comforted herself by collecting some of the younger children around her and telling them stories; they loved it, always asking for more. But all the time the thought of Pauline's going away lay on her like a great weight.

Pauline entered Carmel on October 2, 1882. Her father, Marie, and Monsieur Guérin took her to the convent, while their aunt went with Léonie, Céline, and Thérèse to Mass. They were all crying so much that everyone turned round to look when they came into church, but Thérèse did not care. She wondered how the sun could go on shining.

That afternoon she saw Pauline again, now dressed as a postulant. The new religious name that she had been given, to mark the newness of her life, was Agnes of Jesus. Between Sister Agnes and her sister there was now a double grille of thick iron bars.

7. Breakdown

THAT was only the beginning. Every day Thérèse missed the sister who had been her comforter, adviser, and friend. When the family went to visit their Carmelite, Thérèse had only a few minutes at the end of the visit in which to talk to her sister, instead of the long, intimate conversations for which she longed. Since her mother's death she had never been strong, though she was not cosseted or allowed to stay away from school unless she was really ill. Her unhappiness at school had made matters worse, and the loss of Pauline was the last straw. She did not complain; her determination to carry on as Pauline would wish did not fail, but her health did. By the end of the year 1882, a few months after Pauline had gone, she began to have frequent headaches, which went on until the following Easter. They were just bearable, and she managed to carry on with her schoolwork in spite of them.

Monsieur Martin took Marie and Léonie to Paris for

Holy Week, and Thérèse and Céline went to stay with the Guérins. One evening she had been talking to her uncle about her mother and began to cry quietly, but afterward her headache became suddenly much worse. She began to tremble all over. They put her to bed at once and sent for her father.

By the time he got back from Paris, she was very ill indeed. She saw horrible visions, she screamed and threw herself about so that they had to hold her down to keep her from hurting herself. Her bed seemed to her to have deep precipices all around it, the nails in the wall looked like huge blackened fingers, her father's hat, as he sat by her bed, suddenly seemed to change into some fearful shape.

"Oh—the big black beast!" she cried, her face so twisted with terror that her poor father left the room weeping. Then she would fall into a coma, sometimes for hours, not able to move at all, though she could hear what was said near her.

It seems almost certain that she was having what nowadays we would call a nervous breakdown, and considering what she had been through it isn't very surprising. The family doctor could not do anything at all. He had no idea what caused her illness or how to cure it. Madame Guérin, Marie, and Léonie nursed her and watched over her, but could do nothing to help. Thérèse herself said later that it was surely the devil, jealous of Pauline's vocation, who was taking his revenge on her.

The date fixed for Pauline's clothing was April 6, 1883. Everyone thought Thérèse would be too ill to go, so they never spoke of it in front of her, in case the disappointment should make her worse. But Thérèse said she would go, and when the day came she seemed perfectly well and was allowed to. She was able to see her sister in her beautiful wedding dress when she came out of the convent enclosure into the parlor. She sat on her knee, drew the white veil around her and talked to her favorite sister, but it was not for long. Pauline passed once more through the enclosure door, leaving her outside. The carriage came, and they went home to *Les Buissonnets* again. Next day Thérèse was more ill than ever, and every day she got worse.

Marie stayed with her night and day; the whole household was desperately anxious. She got weaker, and it seemed as if she would die. All through April it dragged on, and into May. It was the month dedicated to Mary, and whenever the fever left her Thérèse liked to make wreaths of daisies and forget-me-nots for Our Lady's statue. It stood on a bracket a few feet above her head, beyond the white bed-curtains, as she lay in her sister's sunny room. But these quiet moments did not last long. At *Les Buissonnets* and at Carmel, at the abbey and in her uncle's home, prayers were offered for her, and at the beginning of May, Monsieur Martin told Marie to write to the church of Our Lady of Victories in Paris to ask that for nine days Masses should be offered there for her cure.

The thirteenth of May was a Sunday. Marie, tired by her weeks of nursing, went out for a short walk in the garden, leaving Léonie in charge. Léonie sat reading by the window, and she heard Thérèse call softly, "Marie! Marie!" Léonie was used to this sort of thing and took no notice, but Thérèse called more loudly, so that Marie came hurrying back. Thérèse saw her come in, but then, suddenly, she did not know who it was and looked around in a worried way, still calling for Marie.

Again and again Marie tried to get Thérèse to recognize her, but it was no good. After a while she went out into the garden and, when Léonie carried Thérèse to the window, held out her arms to her, smiling and calling out, "Thérèse, my darling Thérèse!" But though Thérèse saw someone out there, she still did not know who it was. Pale and shaken, Marie came back to the bedroom. She knelt at the foot of the bed and, with tears pouring down her face, turned toward Our Lady's statue and prayed for her sister's life. Léonie and Céline joined her, and poor Thérèse added her own prayers.

Ever since her mother had died, Thérèse had learned to think of Mary, the Mother of Jesus, as her Mother in Heaven in a special way, so now she asked her, quite naturally, to help her in her bewildering and frightening sickness. Suddenly it seemed to Thérèse that she saw the beauty of Mary herself and that, in place of a statue, Mary smiled at her with a motherly smile that went straight to her heart.

Two big tears trickled down Thérèse's cheeks. They were tears of happiness. Her Mother had come to her, and all the pain had gone. "How happy I am," she thought, "but I mustn't tell anyone or the happiness will go away." Then the vision was gone, but when she lowered her eyes she saw Marie and recognized her at once. Marie had seen her eyes fixed on the statue, and watching the look on her face change from one of pain to one of joy, she guessed that something wonderful had happened. She asked Thérèse, and not wanting to hurt her sister's feelings, Thérèse at last told her about it. But putting her experience into words hurt Thérèse. It seemed somehow to make what she had seen less real, and later on she blamed herself for what she felt was a sort of betrayal. But she was really cured; no trace of the illness remained except a slight giddiness, which soon disappeared. In a day or two, Thérèse was back to her normal daily routine, but she had been delicate before and was still not strong. Her oversensitiveness and her headaches remained to plague her.

Meanwhile, off rushed Marie to Carmel to tell the wonderful news, and although she had meant to tell only Sister Agnes about it, the other nuns told one another the exciting story, so that when Thérèse visited the parlor they were all eager to hear details. She told them what had happened in few words, unwilling to share her great secret, but that wasn't enough for them.

"What was Our Lady wearing?"

"Was she carrying the Holy Child?"

"Were there angels with her?"

There were endless questions, and Thérèse, sensitive and reserved as ever, could not satisfy them. "Our Lady was very beautiful, and she came toward me with a smile." That was all she would say, growing every moment more miserable. She thought she had told the story badly, had made a mistake. She began to wonder whether she had been telling the truth; she even imagined that her illness had been only pretense. As for the nuns, many of them thought she had imagined it all or, worse still, made it up. Their distrust and the exaggerations of her own tortured conscience destroyed all her happiness. For years the memory of that wonderful moment gave her nothing but pain.

After three months' convalescence, Monsieur Martin took Thérèse away for a few weeks' holiday. He had quite a lot of well-to-do friends with big country houses who had often asked him to stay, and now he thought the country air and change of scene would help to make Thérèse quite strong again. It was full summer, and in beautiful weather Thérèse met for the first time the comforts and pleasures of the rich. She had always had pretty clothes—her sisters took great pride in them—but she had been taught that it was wrong to think much about her appearance. Now she was petted, admired, fussed over. Everyone wanted to be kind to the charming little girl who had been ill. The big houses, the beautiful gardens, the long, elaborate meals at tables shining with silver, fine linen, and flowers, the pretty dresses of the ladies, their jewels, scent, carriages, ladies' maids—it all seemed wonderfully exciting and new. Gravely, she watched all these gay people as they ate, walked, rode, played. She listened to their chatter, their jokes, their mild flirtations. It was all great fun, and with it all they went to church on Sundays, they gave alms to the poor. Thérèse had been ill and was still weak, and at first this gave her a curiously far-off point of view, as if the life around her were only a picture she was looking at. She thought about it all, reflecting on what she saw in a pious and slightly smug way, which she had learned from her sisters, but with a lot of ironical common sense. She saw that the churchgoing and almsgiving didn't really mean much; they were just the "done thing." It seemed easy, on the surface, to serve God and pleasure, but the combination didn't seem to work. "I wonder if they even remember they are going to die?" Thérèse asked herself. But she was not self-righteous, and she did enjoy the fun and appreciate the kindness that was lavished on her. Later, she felt glad that she had not stayed longer in the rich, gay world, because as she grew stronger, her own natural gaiety and capacity for enjoyment awoke, and she began to find the life very attractive.

But autumn was coming; it was time to start school again. She had missed a term; there would be a lot to catch up. She was in the third class, and, much more important, now that she was eleven she was to prepare for her first communion.

In the early days of the Church, quite small children had been allowed to receive holy communion. "Why can't they now?" Thérèse often asked, restless at having to wait so long. Since Thérèse's death there have been great changes in the Catholic Church, and Catholics now see much more clearly that communion is an essential part of the Eucharist for all those who take part. People normally receive communion every time they join in the celebration of the Eucharist, and children come to communion as soon as they are old enough to understand the meaning of what they are doing and want to do it. But when Thérèse was a child, communion was infrequent, and children seldom received it until they were eleven. Thérèse's birthday was on January 2, so she had to watch other children whose birthdays were perhaps only a week or so before hers being allowed to make their first communion a whole year earlier than herself.

8. *Communion and Conversion*

B Y THE TIME she went back to school for the autumn term after her illness, the day of communion was only a matter of months away, and she set herself to prepare for it with all her natural single-mindedness. Marie talked it over with her at home in the evening, passing on to her little sister some of her own courage in God's service. Pauline was no longer there to talk to her, but in Carmel she prayed every day for her sister and also gave her a book of prayers and thoughts about holy communion which she had written out herself, and she suggested that Thérèse should write down in it the number of her small sacrifices and prayers, calling them by the names of different flowers to be offered to the Holy Child. It was a rather sentimental idea, but the sacrifices were real enough, and Thérèse made them with a courage that had nothing sentimental about it. More and more she turned to God as her only companion, for apart from the great affection of her family, she had become a lonely little girl since her illness. The news of her wonderful cure had got around; people talked. Her moment of weakness, when she had told Marie about the vision, had to be paid for. Other people now thought of her as specially blessed; she was different from the others, and they left her alone. This was not her doing, for she was naturally a friendly person.

Possibly, though, Thérèse did not really notice this isolation. A great deal was going on in the depths of Thérèse's mind that she did not fully understand. Just as, unnoticed, her body had grown longer as she lay ill in bed, so it seemed as if her mind had been growing, too. She felt desires and hope and fears that she had never known before, undefined longing and discontent sometimes seized her. She needed time and quiet to let these new thoughts and feelings develop. Thérèse asked Marie whether she could keep half an hour a day especially for silent prayer. She did not realize that prayer is, in fact, a name for this growing and stretching of love in the depths of the mind, but she felt intuitively that she needed silence and solitude in the thought and presence of God. But Marie refused. She may have thought it would be too much for a child who was still not very strong, and Thérèse obeyed, or thought she did.

"What do you do on your half-holidays?" asked one of the mistresses at the abbey one day.

Thérèse blushed. "Sometimes I hide myself in a corner of my room which I can shut off with bed-curtains and"—she paused, wondering how to explain—"and just think."

Her mistress laughed. "What do you think about?"

"About God," said Thérèse slowly, "about how short life is, and about eternity, and—well, I just think."

Although she did not know it, she was praying.

Eight days before her great day, she went into retreat at the abbey, living there as a boarder. She loved every minute of it. The nuns were so kind to her, especially kind, she thought, because she had no mother. Every night the Head-mistress, her dear Mother Sainte Placide, passed down the long dormitory with her little lamp, stopping at the white-curtained beds to wish each child good night. At last one night, as the nun bent to kiss her forehead, Thérèse, touched by her kindness, decided to tell her something.

"Madame," she whispered, "I want to tell you a secret." Mother Sainte Placide smiled down at her as Thérèse put her hand under her pillow and pulled out the precious book that Pauline had given her. Shyly she held it out, and the nun opened it and saw the long record of Thérèse's gifts of love. The times when she had been scolded and had not defended herself, had concealed a headache and gone on with her work, had given away her pocket money, played a game she disliked because someone else wanted to—these things, and many others, were disguised in the book as "roses" or "daisies" or "violets."

Mother Sainte Placide understood. She knew that Thérèse needed a great deal of loving and that this had prompted her to show the precious book, but also what was in the book showed that Thérèse was capable of giving a great deal of love. "You're a very lucky little girl," she said, and she gave the book back with a kind smile.

The days passed quietly. The nun who looked after the dormitory was astonished to discover that a big girl of eleven was so accustomed to being waited on that she couldn't even dress without help. Laughing, the nun combed Thérèse's hair for her, not as gently as Marie usually did.

Thérèse must have looked very odd, for she kept a big crucifix stuck in her belt, like a missionary. She was living in a world of her own, peopled by saints and martyrs, and the girls who shared her retreat seemed to her less real than her own thoughts. She listened to the chaplain's talks very carefully and took notes, and she was glad to be able to follow the Psalms and prayers of the divine office with the nuns. Very, very often she thought of Pauline, who was also in retreat because she was going to make her vows in Carmel on the day of Thérèse's first communion.

At last the day came, May 8, 1884. Thérèse woke at dawn and lay quietly, full of happiness, until it was time to get up. All the little girls went to a special room to dress, and there were their white dresses, veils, and wreaths, looking like piles of snowflakes. Thérèse's dress was very simple; the bodice had pleats from neck to waist, and the only other decoration was the soft frilling at the neck and wrists. There was a big sash to go with it, and from the waist hung a little pocket with two bows on it and a white rosary. The nuns and some of the older girls kissed the children tenderly and helped to dress them. Hardly noticing what was happening, Thérèse allowed herself to be buttoned into her dress. The big bow was adjusted, the transparent veil thrown over her head, and the wreath of white roses fixed in position. At last they were all ready, and the procession of small white figures passed sedately into the chapel. As they went to their places, they heard the beginning of a morning hymn to the Blessed Sacrament. The priest came to the altar; the familiar liturgy of the Mass began.

Thérèse could never tell afterward what she thought and felt at that time. It went too deep to be put into words. It was many years now since she had offered her whole life to God. Now she came to the altar rails and for the first time took her full share as a Christian in the action she had watched so often. "The bread which we share," St. Paul had called it, and this sharing was a sharing of love. Jesus loved her, she loved him and gave herself to him; they were no longer two, for it seemed to Thérèse that she had disappeared like a drop of water falling into the sea. He was her Lord and her King; her weakness was filled with his strength. She was filled with a joy so great that she could not bear it, and she began to cry quietly. Tears ran down her face, but tears of perfect happiness.

"What was the matter with Thérèse?" said the little girls to one another afterward. "Do you think she remembered some bad things she'd done?"

"Perhaps she was missing her mother," suggested one.

"Or her Carmelite sister—she loves her so much," said another.

They simply could not understand that anyone could cry for joy. How could she miss her mother when all Heaven had come to her with Our Lord, bringing her darling mother so near to her? And Pauline seemed closer than ever as Thérèse thought of her making her vows to God that same day.

In the afternoon, Thérèse was chosen to read the prayer consecrating all the first communicants to Mary. Possibly Thérèse was chosen because she had lost her earthly mother, and certainly she put all her heart into what she read, asking her Mother to guard her always. Thérèse remembered Our Lady's lovely smile, which had cured her when she was so ill, and thanked her once more.

In the evening, Monsieur Martin took Thérèse to Carmel to see Sister Agnes, now a professed nun and wearing, like Thérèse, a crown of roses. Looking at her, Thérèse longed to be with her, and the hope of following her to Carmel made her happiness even greater.

Home at *Les Buissonnets* they had a little party, and there were presents, one of which was a pretty watch from her father. It was a lovely, peaceful ending to her day. Before she went to bed that night, she wrote down three resolutions in her notebook. "I will never let myself be discouraged," she wrote. "I will say the *Memorare* every day. I will try to humble my pride."

But the days that followed seemed very dreary. She looked

at the pretty dress Marie had given her and at the other presents given by people who loved her, but they did not cheer her up. She was absorbed by her longing for a new meeting with Christ in the Sacrament, and at this time she had not yet learned to give herself fully to Christ in loving other people. That was something that only years and suffering could teach her. Meanwhile she was so entranced by what she had experienced of Christ as the source of all love that she could scarcely see anything or anybody else. There was only one thought in her mind: "How long until I can receive Our Lord once more?" But in those days, ordinary people went to communion on big feast days only, and there seemed to be so few of them. But there was a feast day quite soon, only eight days after Thérèse's first communion.

The night before, Marie helped her again to prepare herself, as she was to do before each feast day. That evening she talked about suffering. "But," she said, "I am sure God will always carry you like a small child—he will not make you walk that road." Next day after communion, Thérèse remembered these words, but they did not please her. She suddenly felt that she wanted to suffer for Our Lord's sake, and she was sure that he would send her plenty of suffering. She was deeply convinced that only suffering, accepted out of love, could open a person entirely to the work of love. In suffering she could show her love and let it grow. This strong desire to suffer is one that many people have felt when they are deeply in love. A person in love is not afraid of pain or difficulties; they are a challenge, an exciting and wonderful opportunity to prove one's love. Thérèse was in love with God—as much in love as anyone could be—so it was natural that she should long to suffer. But she also realized that her own courage was very small. Only the Spirit of God, who is love itself, could rid her of the fears that held her back and give her the courage of perfect love.

The Sacrament of confirmation is especially concerned

with the work of the Spirit. The baptized Christian receives
from the whole Church the commission to be a brave and
loving witness for Christ. For this he needs the gifts that
belong to the Spirit, so the Church prays for him, and the
Bishop, laying his hands on him, passes on to him his commission as a Christian and prays for the strength he needs
to carry it out.

Thérèse began to prepare for her confirmation, which
was to take place on June 14, 1884, quite soon after her
first communion. Again she went into retreat, and when the
ceremony had to be put off for a few days, she was glad of
the extra time to get ready. During this retreat, people who
knew her noticed that there seemed to be a new strength
about her and a kind of deep excitement. Céline was surprised and said so.

"What makes you look like that?" she asked.

"I'm thinking all the time of the great power of the Sacrament," Thérèse answered, her face glowing with enthusiasm.
"I think of how the Holy Spirit will take possession of my
whole self."

Céline never forgot how she looked at that moment and
went away very much moved.

So Thérèse was confirmed and put on "the whole armor
of God" that she was going to need so badly later on.

She returned now to her ordinary school life and worked
very hard. She got on well at lessons, but still found learning
by heart difficult. All the same, she was good at Catechism,
for she was passionately interested in everything to do with
God, and the chaplain nicknamed her "the little doctor"
because she knew so much theology. She seemed old for her
age and lived a more and more lonely life at school. At
break she walked about by herself thinking about serious
things. Even her storytelling had been stopped because it
prevented the girls' getting enough exercise, so one of her

few ways of really living with other people and getting to know them was cut off.

She was making efforts to overcome her sickly shyness and fear of other people, but often her attempts ended badly. She really tried to make friends, and at one time she had two. With one of them she had only a slight friendship, and we don't know what happened to that girl afterward. The other girl had to be away for some months, so Thérèse was very excited over her return and longed to see her. When she got back, she never so much as spoke to Thérèse, just stared at her as if she had never seen her before. It had never occurred to Thérèse that one could suddenly stop loving a person, and she was deeply hurt. She told herself that friendship like that was not worth having, that the only real friendship was love of God and of other people for his sake. But this really meant that, for the time being, she just could not manage to cope with other people's real characters. Her own family protected her and petted her, but even at home she was tearful and moody.

Other girls hero-worshiped one of the mistresses, bringing her flowers and trying to attract her attention. Thérèse thought a little wistfully that it would be nice to do the same, but she was not the kind of girl who would naturally do this, and she was too shy to approach the mistresses in a more direct and friendly way. So she told herself it was silly, anyway, to indulge in this kind of devotion.

In May, 1885, Thérèse and the other girls who had made their first communion the year before made a special solemn communion on the anniversary of their great day. There were no tears of joy this time. For several days Thérèse had been worrying over her every tiny imperfection until each seemed a dreadful sin. She could not make up her mind about a single thing in case she might choose wrongly. These "scruples" sound very silly to people who don't suffer from them, but those who are trying very hard to love God sometimes get this kind of spiritual "illness." Their common sense does not grow as fast as their desire to do everything perfectly for God's sake, and so they get things out of proportion and worry themselves sick over trifles instead of trusting in God. Thérèse got this trouble badly, and it lasted for two years. Every day when she got home from school, Marie would sit her down to curl her hair for the next day (her father liked it curled), and all the time Thérèse kept up a stream of worried questions and moans about her faults. Marie's patience had to be endless.

After the solemn communion, Madame Guérin took Thérèse to Deauville for a holiday with her own family. They went shrimping and rode donkeys as they had always done, and Thérèse loved the sea. The only trouble was that the Chalet Colombe, which they rented, was a long way from the church. Thérèse insisted on going to Mass there every morning, whatever the weather, and to the special prayers to Our Lady every evening during May.

In September, Monsieur Martin left home to go on a long journey with a priest friend of his through Austria, Germany, and Italy, so the girls again went in turn to stay with their aunt at Deauville, in a different house this time. Kind Madame Guérin did everything she could to keep her nieces happy, but because Marie could not be with her, Thérèse was bored. Her aunt bought Thérèse some new hair ribbons—sky-blue ones—which delighted her. But she had no sooner tied up her hair than her pleasure in them began to seem sinful. Ought she to accept such finery? Was she being vain? On the other hand, wouldn't she hurt her aunt's feelings if she didn't wear them? In an agony of doubt, she rushed off to confession in Trouville.

Thérèse was so grown up in her ways that people were inclined to forget that she was still only twelve. She was used to a lot of affection and fuss, for her own family were accustomed to her oversensitiveness, so they protected and comforted her. In the normally easygoing and cheerful atmosphere of the Guérin family, nobody felt it necessary to give her special treatment. Thérèse missed her father and sisters and was very sorry for herself. She longed to be coddled a bit.

Her cousin Marie, who was fourteen, often had headaches and would curl up in a chair and moan and cry, while her mother fussed over her, calling her pet names and coddling her. Thérèse had headaches nearly every day, probably from worrying over imaginary sins, but she hadn't said anything about them.

One evening she thought she'd try it too. She curled up in an armchair and moaned. Her older cousin Jeanne and her aunt both came running to ask what was the matter.

"Oh! My poor head!" complained Thérèse, but they just did not believe her.

"I suppose you are worrying over some fearful scruple, as usual, and don't want to tell your aunt," said Jeanne a little impatiently. She was rather tired of Thérèse's scruples. "I must say I think you might have trusted her and told her the real reason!"

Thérèse gave it up. In spite of her self-pity, she had a strong sense of humor even about herself. She suddenly remembered a rhyme she had learned at school about a donkey who put his hooves on the table hoping to be petted like the little dog. All he got was a good clout. And, thought Thérèse, if I was not actually beaten, like the poor donkey, I was certainly punished as I deserved! I shan't ever try to attract attention again!

But though she got no sympathy for her headaches, they were there just the same—and getting worse. She went back to school in October, alone now, for Céline had left school. She worked hard, but her health was obviously suffering, and her father took her away from school at the end of the autumn term. He arranged for her to have lessons several times a week with a lady who lived near.

It was a very odd arrangement, for Madame Papineau, as her name was, taught Thérèse in her own parlor, where her old mother sat and where lessons were enlivened by a constant stream of visitors. Most of them talked to Madame Papineau's mother, but although Thérèse kept her nose well down in her books, she could not help hearing what they said, even through the purring of the cat, which was allowed to sit on her exercise books.

"Who is the charming new pupil?"

"What a pretty girl!"

"What beautiful hair!"

Thérèse was secretly flattered and pleased, but her oversensitive conscience made her afraid that she might become vain. She felt that the example of Mary, the Mother of Jesus, would be a help to her, for Mary was the most privileged woman who had ever lived, yet she lived as an ordinary workingman's wife. Thérèse decided to join a group called the Children of Mary. They were a group of women and girls especially dedicated to following Mary's example by prayer and charitable work, and there was a group of them in Lisieux which met at the abbey. To do this she had to go through a year of probation, during which she had to attend a sewing class twice a week at the abbey. Her shyness made these classes dreadful to her. She had no friends among the other girls, so she worked on quietly by herself until the end of the hour and then, hoping no one noticed her, slipped up to the chapel to wait until her father came to fetch her. Of course, this meant that one of the purposes of joining the group, which was to work *together* for God, was defeated. But Thérèse could not bring herself to overcome her shyness yet. One of the girls did notice and admire her, for in spite of her retiring manner, she could not help being an attractive person. This girl wanted to make friends and used to wait for her after class, but Thérèse was too quick and was in the chapel before the other girl could get to her. She often stayed there more than an hour.

So next year, 1887, she became a Child of Mary. She went on with her lessons, and life at *Les Buissonnets* continued on its way with its routine of walks, work, reading, and prayer. Céline took care of the room they shared, for Thérèse was still doing lessons and was not expected to do housework, although most girls of her age would have had their share. Sometimes she exerted herself to make the bed or to fetch Céline's little plants and cuttings from the garden if Céline was out, and she truly thought that she did this "for the love of God," but she did not understand that real love of God is love of other people, and service of others for God's sake is worthless if it is not given out of real love for real people. She herself craved for human love, and her little acts of service were really a plea for love. So if Céline did not show that she was surprised or say thank you, Thérèse sat down and cried. She cried if she hurt someone's feelings by accident until she made herself ill. When she felt better, she cried again—for having cried before.

Then, suddenly, came another shock: Marie was to enter Carmel, too. Thérèse would soon be fourteen; she could stand it now, thought Marie, and Thérèse did not blame her. But who now would untangle her scruples for her when she had worried herself into knots? Who would listen patiently and set her mind at rest, at least for the moment? She sat down and cried. But that did not help, and as there was no one on earth who could help her, she suddenly thought of her little brothers and sisters in Heaven. If they had lived, they would have wanted to help her, so why shouldn't they do so now? Unable to talk of her trouble to the people around her, she found some comfort in imaginary talks to Marie-Hélène, to Marie-Joseph Louis, to Marie-Joseph Jean-Baptiste, to Marie-Mélanie Thérèse. She begged them to pray that the scruples which made her life a misery might be cured.

And talking to them did help. The thought of these children, knowing God in the fullness of peace, brought peace to Thérèse's anxious soul, and in the knowledge of God's love her scruples melted away.

But the foolish oversensitiveness remained—she still cried for any or no reason. All through her life, as soon as she learned to love someone and rely on her, she had been snatched from her: her foster-mother; then her real mother; then Pauline, her "little mother"; and now Marie—strict but just and loving—had gone, too. She was unable to make friends, unable to confide her troubles, and she was tormented by constant headaches as a result of all this worrying. Thérèse's tearfulness was the inevitable result of what was wrong with her and is not at all surprising. But a really surprising thing did happen to Thérèse just before she was fourteen.

It was Christmas, 1886, and Thérèse was almost fourteen. Coming home from midnight Mass, the Martins found the great fire blazing cheerfully in the hearth and in front of it the shoes stuffed with presents such as Thérèse had had every Christmas, as far back as she could remember. She rushed upstairs to take her things off before opening her presents, and as she went she heard her father's voice as he spoke to Léonie. "Thérèse ought to have outgrown this sort of thing," he said impatiently. "I hope this will be the last time." Thérèse, standing on the dark stairs, was deeply hurt, and Céline, coming up behind her, whispered quickly, "Don't go down again just yet. You will only go and cry if you open your presents now in front of Father."

But Céline was speaking to a Thérèse who had, in that moment, ceased to exist. It was as if the desire to be strong and brave that had been struggling for so long against the weight of fear now suddenly broke through. It was a severe shock to hear her father's impatient tone, so unlike his usual gentleness to her. She realized in a moment that she had been protected by her own self-pity and her family's devotion from realizing that she was nearly grown up, with a grown-up person's responsibilities. She had been about to make a scene over some toys and candies! If Thérèse had not been a really loving and brave person, a shock like this might only have made her more withdrawn and more sorry for herself. But she truly did want to love, and in that moment she was able to. The power of love that Christians call grace simply swept away the rubbish of self-pity.

Thérèse took off her outdoor things, dried the tears that still stood in her eyes, and ran down to the dining room. She picked up the shoes and unwrapped her presents, looking as happy as if nothing had happened. Her father had forgotten his annoyance and enjoyed it all, too, while Céline stood by, unable to believe her eyes.

9. *The* *Call*

THE PRIEST finished the last Gospel and turned to leave the altar, and the congregation knelt down. Thérèse closed her missal, and as she did so a picture of the crucifixion slipped out a little way. She looked down and saw one of Our Lord's hands, held to the wood by a great nail while the blood flowed down unchecked, that blood that was shed for the saving of souls. It runs down, thought Thérèse, and no one bothers to catch it. A great wave of feeling swept over her, and there and then she offered herself to God to stand always at the foot of the cross, to receive the blood of her Savior and pour it out upon the souls who needed it so much. The blood of Christ was for her an image of the love that drove him to face death. It was this love that she, Thérèse, must give to all the people who lived in fear and hopelessness because they did not know that they were loved. Thérèse was now fourteen, and she realized at last that a love of God that wraps itself in remoteness from other people is not real love at all. To love Christ was to share his untiring love for human beings, even to death.

Thérèse set about putting this understanding into practice with all her natural energy. She who had been such a little crybaby was now a pleasure to have in the family. Nothing was too much trouble; she was always courteous, even-tempered, and helpful. She was particularly nice to the servants, for she noticed how often people were careless or unkind to those who worked for them. People found it easy to talk to Thérèse about spiritual things because she so clearly thought of nothing else herself. She used to talk quietly about God's goodness to us and of how we ought to love him very much in return. Madame Guérin's maid, who loved to listen to her, was worried by this.

"I don't feel that love at all, Miss Thérèse," she confessed sadly.

"Oh, but you don't understand," answered Thérèse. "It's not the *feeling* that matters. You don't have to *feel* love for God. It's doing good for his sake that counts."

But she could not talk to everyone about God, and for these other people she prayed and prayed. The girls weren't supposed to read newspapers, but Monsieur Martin discussed with them what went on in the world and at one time talked of a notorious murderer called Pranzini, who had been condemned to death for killing two women and a little girl. He was not in the least ashamed of what he had done. He refused to see a priest, and even the nearness of death seemed to have no effect on him. Thérèse was horrified. To die without repentance, in willful rebellion against God —that meant that all that Christ had suffered for him was useless. How could she bear it? She would not bear it. She decided to save Pranzini from the hell to which he was condemning himself.

Thérèse could not rush off to throw herself at his feet and plead with him. Even if she had got there, it would probably have done no good. But what she couldn't do, God could do. She prayed. She thought about Christ's death, about the Resurrection, which let loose the power of his love, and about the Eucharist, in which Christians come together so that they may share in that love and grow in it and give it. She prayed that the power of this love would reach even a man like Pranzini. Indeed, she could not believe that love like that could possibly fail, but she was child enough, still, to long for a little reassurance, some sign that love did indeed work wonders like this. Half-laughing at herself, she prayed, "O God, I am sure you are going to forgive poor Pranzini, and I trust so greatly in your mercy that I shall go on being sure—even if he does not go to confession or show any sign at all of being sorry. But because he is my first sinner, please give me just one sign to let me know."

The morning after the execution, Thérèse decided it would not be disobedient to look at the paper. (She was still always sure that what she wanted very much must be right.) She could hardly wait to get it and read the account of Pranzini's death. He had gone to the scaffold still refusing absolution, said the account in the newspaper, hard and bitter to the end. He was roped to the guillotine, and the knife was about to fall, when he suddenly turned his head to where the prison chaplain stood and asked for the crucifix, which he kissed three times. Then the knife fell. Thérèse left the room in a hurry, to calm down before meeting the others. It was the sign for which she had asked. It was the sight of Christ's wounded hand which had filled her with the longing to save souls, and it was on those wounds that the lips of her "first child" had been pressed. It was a wonderful answer, and her desire to love grew greater and greater.

Thérèse was intelligent and hardworking, but up to the time of her "conversion," her mind had been hampered by the weight of her fears and worries. Released from this burden, she suddenly found herself impatient for knowledge. She was so eager to learn that her teacher could hardly keep up with her. She read a great deal at home as well, sitting at a table in her room that looked over the park, studying so eagerly and so fast that she learned more in a few months than she had ever done at school. This sudden terrific thirst for all kinds of learning might have used up all her energy, and caused her to lose her sense of the things that matter most. She knew that knowledge is important in order to form a human being who is able to love with all his powers and talents. She carried a copy of *The Imitation of Christ* with her wherever she went and read it so much that she knew most of it by heart. This account of how a Christian should order his life in the service of God was written by a Flemish monk some five hundred years ago. In it Thérèse found a chapter warning the good Christian against running after knowledge for its own sake or out of vanity, and she took that warning to heart.

Céline, who had been her friend when she was still a little girl, was now even more closely her companion, the one to whom she could talk easily, naturally. Both of them wanted God above all things. During this time, they were learning together to love him, and what they discovered and discussed in their long talks helped both of them through the difficulties ahead. In the evenings they sat together in the attic room, watching the coming night deepen the blue of the sky and scatter it with stars. Heaven seemed only a step or two away. What did earthly things matter? Only one thing mattered: to love God with one's whole heart.

Thérèse gradually found self-discipline easier. At first the struggle to conquer herself showed in her face, but after a time she managed to hide the effort. Her daily life was lived very close to God, and now she was allowed by her confessor to go to communion several times a week. Day by day, Thérèse longed more and more to give herself com-

pletely to God. How? Where? Everything pointed the way to
Carmel. She would have liked to be a missionary, to bring
the good news of the Gospel to those who had never known
it, or to work among the poor or the sick, but she felt that
the best way of all to win souls for God is by prayer and
sacrifice. In Carmel she could sacrifice herself completely,
alone and in silence.

Thérèse was in love, and the Carmelite life seemed to her
the most perfect gift of love that she could make—not for
her own sake, but for the sake of Christ, who gave himself
out of love. But like most people in love, she was blind to
everything but the one thing she wanted. Also she was very
young and had the headstrong impetuousness of her age,
backed by a very strong will. She did not, as people thinking
of religious life often do, consult a sensible priest. She never
felt the need of one, for she was sure that Christ himself was
guiding her. Every time she went to visit her sisters at the
convent, she spoke of her longing to enter. Marie said she
was far too young, but Pauline encouraged her all the time.
At first she said nothing to Céline, because she knew she
wanted to be a nun, too, and it did not seem fair that Thérèse,
so much younger, should go first. But Céline soon guessed
what was the matter. So with great courage and unselfishness,
she told Thérèse to go ahead and helped her in every way
she could. Then, almost before she knew where things were
leading, Thérèse found herself faced with the most difficult
task she had ever undertaken: she must tell her father of
her vocation.

He was getting old, sixty-four now. Earlier that year he
had had a stroke one morning and had been very ill, though
he had insisted on going to Mass just the same. He got better,
and he looked healthy enough, but had two more attacks
afterward, and would probably have more. He had not many
more years of life left. Thérèse was only a child still. Surely

he could expect her to be his companion for those few years, before she gave herself to God in the convent? She was his joy, the one he loved best, his "little queen." How could she tell him that God was calling her away from him? Surely it would break his heart. But she felt she had to do it—she was quite sure that what she wanted was God's will.

The feast of Pentecost was coming, when the Holy Spirit gave to the Apostles who had run away from their Lord the courage to go out and face death joyfully in order to bring the good news of Christ to the world. Thérèse felt it was a suitable day for her undertaking. All day she prayed for the gifts of the Spirit, and she asked the Apostles to pray for her, to give her the right words when the time came.

Monsieur Martin sat in the garden, watching the sunset behind the trees catch the leaves in a last brilliance so that the whole garden seemed alight with golden fire. Out of the house came Thérèse, and he turned to watch her come, glad to share the calm of the evening with his favorite daughter. How tall she was, almost a woman, and growing daily more lovely in his eyes, with a shining loveliness that seemed to come from something inside her. Everyone noticed it, more than her beautiful skin or the waterfall of golden hair that was now caught by the sun so that it, too, seemed on fire. But as she came nearer, he saw that there were tears in her eyes. Clearly she was upset about something. She sat beside him, unable to speak, and gently he put his arm round her.

"What is it, little queen? Tell me."

Before she could answer, he seemed to feel what was coming, and he got up, still holding her close to him as they walked slowly up the path. Then she told him that she knew she was called to Carmel and how much she longed to enter soon. For a moment the thought of losing his dearest friend and companion was too great a pain. But it was only for a moment. He said nothing to try to keep her for himself, only a gentle word of warning: "You are still very young to decide an important thing like that."

But Thérèse knew her own mind, and she told him all that she had thought and prayed and longed for. She had never seriously thought of any other life but that of the "desert" of Carmel. In her mind there was no doubt at all: her whole will was bent to that one end. And all this her father saw. He wanted only to do whatever she wished, just as he had when she was a baby, and he was willing to help her in every way he could.

For a long time they walked up and down the garden, talking it over, while the sun sank behind the hills. A last ray of light picked out a clump of tiny white flowers shaped like lilies that grew in a crack of a low wall. Monsieur Martin picked one and gave it to his daughter, telling her how God had cared for it and made it bloom and kept it safe. She was like that flower, he said, and now she also was to be pulled up and planted in another garden, the garden of Carmel. And, indeed, as Thérèse took the flower she saw that the roots of the tiny plant had been pulled up with it. It was all ready to begin growing again somewhere else.

If Thérèse thought her troubles were over, she soon found out her mistake. Since her mother's death, her uncle, Monsieur Guérin, had been her legal guardian with her father, and when he heard about this extraordinary plan, he was horrified.

"It's against all good sense," said he, "a girl of fifteen entering a strict Order like that! It would do great harm if a child were allowed to take on a life of that kind. As far as I'm concerned, I refuse to allow it, and only a miracle will make me change my mind!"

It was no use arguing. Thérèse left the house feeling as black and depressed as the weather, for the clouds were dark over the whole sky, and it poured. Her misery lasted for three days, and she was finding out for the first time what it was like to feel that God had left her. Through all the time of her illness and scruples and her unhappiness at school, her one consolation had been the nearness of her Lord, holding her up, consoling her, making the hard things easier. Now she had been given back her strength; she must learn to do without that help. And at this first obstacle on the way to Carmel, she found no comfort in the thought of God. She prayed, and Heaven seemed shut to her prayers; she looked for her Lord to console her, and he was not there. There was nothing but darkness all around her; she was left to struggle on alone. She knew that God had not really deserted her, and never would, but she could not feel this.

On the fourth day, she went to see her uncle again. He met her in the hall, and took her straight to his study. "I don't need a miracle any more," he said. "I asked God to show me his will, and my prayer has been answered. I know that God is calling you to Carmel." He kissed her very kindly, and when she left: "Go in peace, my dear child," he said. "You are a small flower whom Our Lord has chosen, and he wants to gather you for himself. I will not try to stop you any more." The sky was blue, Thérèse was happy again, the darkness had gone.

The next thing was to apply to the convent. Mother Marie Gonzaga, the Prioress, had known Thérèse since she was a little girl. It was to her that Thérèse had brought the news of her vocation when she was nine years old. That was a long time ago, and if it had seemed half a joke then, Mother Marie knew more of Thérèse now, both from talking to her and from her two sisters in Carmel. She knew of what stuff Thérèse was made—she would have been glad to receive her at once. But she had to ask permission from the Superior of Carmel, the priest of St. Jacques, who was appointed by the Bishop to be in charge of the convent.

Canon Delatröette was his name, a good man but very

strict and obstinate. He liked everything nicely ruled and arranged. So when Mother Marie asked about Thérèse: "No," said he, "not until she's twenty-one!" And that was that. There was no Carmelite rule which stopped people from entering before twenty-one, but he had said it, and he stuck to it. Next time he called at the convent to see old Mother Geneviève, who years ago had founded the convent and was now ill in the infirmary, the Prioress asked her to see whether she could persuade him to admit little Thérèse Martin. Mother Geneviève was a very holy woman, and she knew enough of Thérèse to be sure that they needed her in Carmel as much as she wanted to come in, so she did her best.

Canon Delatröette was furious. "Always talking about that girl!" he roared at her. "To hear you talk, one would think the well-being of the community depended on that child's coming here. There's no danger in making her wait a bit. Let her stay at home with her father until she's twenty-one. Do you think I've decided this without praying to God? Don't let me hear anything more about this business!"

When Thérèse heard this, she decided to go and see him herself, and her father went too to give her courage.

She was desperately nervous, though she did not show it. But in any case it was no good. "No!" said he, as soon as she opened her mouth. He went on saying "No!" to all her pleading and arguing. But as they left, he added, "Of course, I'm only acting for the Bishop. If he says you can enter, I cannot stop you."

As they left the Canon's house, the rain came down in torrents.

When they got home, Monsieur Martin wrote to the Bishop to ask for an interview, but they had to wait several months for it. Ordinary life went on. Thérèse had to force herself to be patient. She learned to leave everything in God's hands. She was doing all she could—the rest was up to him. It was very hard, this waiting, but having to wait, and wait cheerfully, matured her as no quick success with her plans could have done.

She was growing fast from a child into a young woman, a brave and firm and loving woman. She did not, as some girls might have done, waste time pretending to be a nun before she was one. She was still in the world, and while she was there she would work for God in the world. Her father had always given her an example in working for the poor and sick; now, when she was not doing her lessons, she spent much of her time in this kind of work. A poor woman became ill, and Thérèse took charge of her two little girls, who had no one to look after them. She talked about the Child Jesus and about Heaven. They listened to every word that the "tall young lady" spoke, and the older one, who was six, asked endless questions. There was no need to bribe them with cakes or candy to make them be kind to each other. Thérèse's words about the joy of Heaven made that seem much more important. She would always be kind to her sister, promised the elder one earnestly. She would never forget what the "tall young lady" had said. But it was not so much what Thérèse said that impressed people as what she was. She talked about her faith in conventional or sentimental words and images—they were the only ones she knew—but her enthusiasm and conviction broke through the stiff words and reached the people who heard her, especially children. Children often know that a person is holy, when older people do not notice.

At last the day came, October 31, 1887. Thérèse and her father went to Bayeux. It was the first time she had gone calling without her sisters, and then to be calling on the Bishop! Trying to look older, she put up her hair in a round bun on top of her head. It certainly felt strange; she hoped it looked impressive, for she felt rather wobbly at the knees. It was not just a matter of answering questions—she would have to explain everything herself. She was dreadfully nervous, but she must conquer her fears. She was no longer Thérèse the crybaby, Thérèse the shy little mouse, but a young woman fighting for something precious that was worth any struggle.

To add to her misery, they were early; and as it was raining, Monsieur Martin took shelter in the cathedral, where a grand funeral was going on. In her light-colored dress and hat, Thérèse felt horribly conspicuous, so that when they finally arrived at the Bishop's house, after many delays, she was in a state of near panic. But in fact everyone was most kind.

Father Révérony, the Vicar-General and the Bishop's adviser, had quick eyes and noticed tears in hers. "You must not show those to his Grace," he said gently.

The huge rooms made Thérèse feel like an ant. How would she be brave enough to open her mouth? Monseigneur Hugonin, Bishop of Bayeux, came to see them in a room where there was a cheerful fire with armchairs in front of it. After they had kissed the Bishop's ring, they were asked to sit down, and Father Révérony offered Thérèse a huge chair in the middle, right in front of the fire. Thérèse excused herself politely, but he insisted. "Show that you can obey!" he said, and Thérèse sat down at once. There would have been room for four people of Thérèse's size to sit comfortably in that chair, much more comfortably than Thérèse at that moment. She had hoped that her father would explain matters, but he left it all to her. She took a breath and plunged in, putting her whole heart into what she said. She was desperately in earnest, and yet these two kindly men really thought it all rather a joke.

"Have you wanted to enter Carmel for a long time?" asked the Bishop after a while.

"Yes, my lord, a very long time!"

Father Révérony laughed. "Come now," he teased, "it cannot have been as much as fifteen years!"

But Thérèse was in no mood for joking. "That's quite true," she said seriously, " but it is not much less. I've wanted to give myself to God since I was three. I've wanted to be a Carmelite ever since I knew about them, because in that Order I think all my desires will be satisfied."

When the Bishop suggested that she ought to stay at home a while longer for her father's sake, he himself broke in to support his daughter. "We shall soon be going on the pilgrimage to Rome from this diocese," he said. "I know my daughter will not hesitate to speak to the Holy Father himself if permission has not been granted by then."

But all that his Lordship would say was that he would speak to the Superior of Carmel about it, and Thérèse knew all too well what his reply would be: "No!" It was the last straw; her courage collapsed, and she cried.

The Bishop did his best to cheer her up. "There's still hope," he said kindly. "I am very pleased that you are going to Rome with your father. It will make your vocation stronger. You ought to be glad, not miserable. I am going to Lisieux next week, and I will talk to the Superior about what you want to do and send my answer to you in Italy."

Then he took them into the garden, and Monsieur Martin added to his daughter's embarrassment by telling the Bishop how she had put up her hair that morning so as to look older. Thérèse wished the earth would swallow her up.

They went back to Lisieux, and Carmel seemed farther off than ever. But there was the pilgrimage to look forward to, and if everything else failed, there was the last hope at Rome. In spite of her sadness, she was at peace.

10. *The* R*oad* *to* R*ome*

AT THREE O'CLOCK in the morning on November 4, 1887, Monsieur Martin, Céline, and Thérèse drove off through the dark streets of Lisieux to the station to begin their pilgrimage to Rome.

Léonie did not come with them. A little while before, when they were on a visit to Alençon, she had suddenly slipped away and asked to be admitted to the convent of Poor Clares. Her family were upset—it was all so sudden—but Léonie was like that, and they hoped very much that she would be happy there. Certainly she had never been very happy at home, for she was moody and not easy to get on with. Even Thérèse found her difficult, and Léonie lived a rather lonely life. Marie and Pauline had always been friends and now had left home; Céline turned always to Thérèse; Léonie was odd man out.

It is odd and sad to notice how seldom Thérèse mentioned Léonie in the childhood reminiscences she wrote later.

Léonie had never felt herself really part of the family, and her hasty entrance into a convent was more a flight from loneliness at home than a response to a vocation. Much later, in a different convent, Léonie found peace, but meanwhile she had the bitterness of knowing that her absence would not cause the grief to her family that the departure of Pauline and Marie had inflicted. It is a symptom of her isolation that she never thought of trying to join her older sisters in the Lisieux Carmel, but chose a convent in another town. So, in the Alençon convent, Léonie struggled with the hard rule and her bad health, while the others set off on their great journey.

The three Martins were to join the other pilgrims in Paris, and they spent three days there seeing the sights. Thérèse did not enjoy it very much. She was itching to begin their real journey, which might decide her fate. But one thing she did remember—a visit to the famous church of Our Lady of Victories. While she knelt at Our Lady's shrine, surrounded by a garden of little candles, it suddenly became quite clear to her that it really was the Mother of Christ who had smiled on her and whose prayers had obtained her cure when she was ill. She asked Our Lady to look after her during the pilgrimage. She was going, for the first time, to meet all sorts of people, to see all kinds of places, she who had never been farther than the seaside with her aunt, and she was afraid of unknown and evil things that she might discover.

On November 7, all the pilgrims gathered in the basilica of the Sacred Heart, which stands on the hill of Montmartre looking over the whole city, like a palace in the *Arabian Nights*. In this great church the Blessed Sacrament can be seen exposed in a gold monstrance, and people come at any hour of the day or night to pray for France. Here the pilgrims prayed before they went to join the train for Switzerland.

There were a lot of rich and titled people on this pilgrimage, which came from two different dioceses. They were making the pilgrimage to honor the fiftieth year as a priest of the Pope, Leo XIII. He was living more or less a prisoner in the Vatican City as a protest against the anti-Catholic actions of the Italian government. The pilgrims wanted to show that the Catholics of France were still loyal to him in spite of everything. Thérèse, usually so shy, got on very well with all these distinguished people and found it quite easy to talk to them.

It was arranged that the pilgrims should have a chance to see many of the lovely Italian cities on their way, and this particularly pleased Monsieur Martin, who loved traveling. Altogether it was a very comfortable sort of pilgrimage, with good trains, excellent hotels all booked, and sightseeing trips arranged. The compartments in the train each had a special patron saint, and the priest who arranged this told the three from Lisieux that their compartment would be called after St. Martin. Monsieur Martin was very pleased at this kind idea, and several people who had heard jokingly called him Monsieur St. Martin.

The first part of the journey was dull. There was no very exciting scenery to look at, and some of the people in the Martins' compartment spent the time playing cards. Thérèse and Céline were worried, for they had been brought up to feel that cardplaying, though not exactly sinful, was rather "fast." Much embarrassed, they made the excuse that they did not know the game. The players were annoyed, and Monsieur Martin stepped in to defend his daughters. "It might be more suitable on a pilgrimage if we gave more time to prayer," he said gently. Monsieur Martin lived so much in his own peaceful world of prayer and good works that he said things like this quite unselfconsciously, as he might gently have reproved one of his daughters if she had been guilty of some small fault. But it was not surprising that the cardplayers, who came from a very different kind of society, were annoyed by what they considered a self-righteous "bourgeois" piety.

"Thank God there are not many such Pharisees about!" shouted one of them rudely. But later on he was ashamed, for Monsieur Martin went out of his way to be nice to him, as if he had not heard.

The train passed through Switzerland after a few hours' stop at Basel. They left there at night, and it was not until they reached the Lake of the Four Cantons (Lake Lucerne) that morning broke. Then Céline and Thérèse glued themselves to the carriage windows, open-mouthed and breathless with excitement. The train rushed along the steep sides of the valleys, and far below they could see torrents of foaming icy water from the glaciers rushing between tall cliffs of rock and under the overhanging ferns and trees, where bunches of red rowanberries dipped to meet the spray. As the valleys opened out, they saw tiny villages where a church spire rose among the steep roofs. Wooden chalets were scattered high on the slopes above, with cows grazing around them. Trails of cloud wound lazily among the high Alps, hiding them from view until, now and then, a gap in the cloud showed a towering ridge dazzling white with snow. Then, as they came around a curve of the mountain, a great lake opened before them, glittering gold in the sunrise. Later on, thought Thérèse, when I am in Carmel, I shall only be able to see a little corner of the sky. I will remember this, and the thought of God's majesty and greatness will put my own small troubles in their place.

They passed through the St. Gothard tunnel and on into Italy, where the plains of Lombardy opened out before them, and the beautiful Italian lakes, with shuttered, tile-roofed houses on their shores painted in pinks and blues and mauves. They came to Milan as dark was falling and were to stay there for some sight-seeing.

While they were there, the two girls climbed all the stairs
to the topmost tower of the Duomo, Milan's great cathedral,
until they could see the whole city below them and the
countryside around. The people below looked like tiny ants.

Thérèse knew nothing about art, and naturally she shared
the taste of the people among whom she lived. She thought
the white marble statues on the graves in Milan's huge cemetery were wonderful; they seemed so real, she thought, that
they almost seemed to move, and all three Martins were lost
in admiration of the dreadful things. One old gentleman
there did not like them, though whether it was because he
saw how bad they were or just because he wanted something
to grouse about, it is impossible to tell. "What keen types
these French people are," he said crossly, though he was
French himself. At least he gave Céline and Thérèse a lot
of amusement, for he never stopped grumbling. He thought
the train was stuffy, the towns ugly, the beds uncomfortable,
the food bad. Why didn't he stay at home, thought Thérèse,
since he clearly was not enjoying himself? But some people
rather enjoy grumbling; possibly he found the "keenness"
of the Martin girls a bit trying, and he was not at all grateful
to Monsieur Martin for trying to cheer him up, offering him
his seat in the train, and making cheerful conversation. He
went on enjoying being miserable all the way to Venice.

Many people think that Venice is the most beautiful city
in the world, with its marble palaces reflected in the water
of the canals, its lovely bridges, its churches full of glowing
pictures and mosaics. Away from the Grand Canal, there
is no noise of traffic, only the gentle lap of water against
weed-grown stones as a gondola passes down the little
canals, where the strips of blue sky seem so far up between
the tall houses. But it is somehow rather a sad city, and so
Thérèse found it. They saw the Palace of the Doges, with
its huge rooms whose walls are covered with paintings.
Thérèse never noticed them. She remembered the horrible

prisons, though, where the Doges' prisoners were shut up for years, perhaps all their lives, and she shuddered as they crossed the Bridge of Sighs, connecting the palace with the prisons.

On they went through Italy, seeing some of the most beautiful buildings that have ever been built and pictures that are so famous the world over that people will save up for years for the chance of seeing them. Traveling in Italy had long been regarded as an education in itself for English and French people, and by the time Thérèse went there it was increasingly fashionable for American tourists also to go there, to admire the buildings and sculptures and paintings and acquire a knowledge of this heart of European culture. Many really understood and appreciated what they saw, others just pretended to, and there were people of both kinds also in the fashionable French pilgrimage that the Martins had joined. But Thérèse did not fit into either category. She was simply not interested. She was thinking about Rome and her vocation; nothing else mattered.

Padua, Bologna, then Loreto—and here she woke up a bit, because in this little mountain town stands the tiny house that a legend says angels brought from Palestine (but which may have been brought by some monks), the Holy House of Nazareth. Thérèse naturally believed the legend and was thrilled to see the home where the Christ had grown up. There were no grand shops in Loreto, no fashionable ladies, only the Italian peasants in their own lovely costumes. Thérèse sighed with relief, for she was beginning to be bored by "society." The Holy House is now inside a huge church, where the pilgrims went to hear Mass. Céline and Thérèse wanted something more than that, though. They wanted to hear Mass and receive communion at the little altar in the Holy House itself, and they were lucky enough to find a priest who was just going to say Mass there.

They left Loreto in the evening, traveling past little villages among pine and yew trees on the slopes of the rounded hills. Thérèse was asleep in her corner of the carriage when the train jolted to a stop and she heard porters run along the train crying, "Roma, Roma!" They had arrived at last.

They stayed at a huge hotel, and while they were there Thérèse noticed that Father Révérony, who was in charge of the pilgrims from Bayeux, was keeping a strict eye on her. He had done so from the start; he was always looking at her, at meals, on sight-seeing trips. If he was not near her, he would move to get a better view. It was very uncomfortable for her, for she knew how much depended on what he told the Bishop about her, but she managed to enjoy herself all the same.

The first day, they explored outside the walls of the city and looked at the Colosseum, which thrilled her. This was where the martyrs had died, and the two girls longed to kiss the ground where those brave men and women had suffered for Christ. But when they got there the guide told them that the original soil of the amphitheater had been buried, in time, twenty-five feet deep. In the middle, excavations were going on; the earth had been dug away in one place right down to the old level, and there were barriers around the hole for safety. Thérèse leaned over the edge.

"Look," she said suddenly to Céline. "There *is* a way down! Follow me!" And without another word the two of them scrambled under the barricade, long skirts, feathered hats, and all, and half-slid, half-climbed down among the rubble and broken walls.

Céline had her wits about her. "The guide said the place of martyrdom was marked by a stone with a cross on it," she said breathlessly when they reached the bottom. They set out to look for it and finally found it.

Thérèse knelt and looked down at the earth. This was where the martyrs had shed their blood for Christ, where they had stood and faced wild beasts, terrified but steadfast in the love for which she also wanted to offer her life. She bent and kissed the ground, her heart thumping with excitement and longing. "Let me be a martyr, too," she whispered, and felt sure that somehow her prayer would be answered.

The round of sight-seeing went on. The idea was to cram into six days all the best sights of the Holy City, so of course they scurried from one great church to another, from the Catacombs to the great Lateran Basilica, the Mother Church of the Christian world; from the old Roman Forum to the Mamertine Prison, where so many Christians had waited for death. Céline and Thérèse saw St. Cecilia's tomb in the Catacombs, and in turn they lay down in this narrow place where her body had been discovered. Perhaps it was the Catacombs that Thérèse liked best, those winding, dimly lit passages and rooms where the first Christians buried those who had died for Christ and met in secret to celebrate the Eucharist, knowing that death was certain if they were found.

It poured with rain, and sight-seeing cannot have been much fun. But Thérèse was thrilled to see the relics of Christ's Passion in the church of the Holy Cross of Jerusalem and was even allowed to put in a finger and touch the nail which, according to tradition, had once been stained with the blood of Christ. One thing really annoyed her: there were so many places where women could not go, so many things women must not do! "They are always saying to us: 'You must not go here, you must not go there, you will be excommunicated!'" she wrote later. "How they despise women! And yet many more women than men love God, and during the Passion of Our Lord the women showed more courage than the Apostles. They endured the insults of the soldiers and dared to wipe the adorable face of Jesus. Because he chose to be despised, he allows women to suffer the same fate during their earthly life. But in Heaven he will show that his ideas are not those of men, for then the last shall be first!"

But the thing that chiefly filled her thoughts was the visit to the Holy Father, which was fixed for the last day of their stay in Rome. It was a Sunday, pouring with rain once more. In long black dresses and heavy lace mantillas they came to the Pope's private chapel for his Mass at eight o'clock. It was wonderful to watch him, pale and thin as he was, attending only to the Lord, whom he served. He spoke slowly, and he meant every word. They felt they were watching a man of real sanctity. As they stood up, Thérèse saw in her missal the words from the day's Gospel: "Fear not, little flock, for it has pleased your Father to give you a kingdom." The kingdom of Carmel, thought Thérèse. Surely everything would be all right.

After another Mass to give thanks, said by one of the chaplains, they went into a great hall, where the audience was to be held. The Holy Father sat in an ordinary armchair up one or two steps, dressed in a white soutane and skullcap; and as each pilgrim came and knelt before him, the priest in charge told the Pope his or her name and anything else that might interest him. He leaned forward and took the hand of each one, spoke a few kindly words, and gave his blessing and a little medal as a souvenir.

Father Révérony presented the Bayeux pilgrims one by one and told the Pope that Monsieur Martin was the father of two Carmelites, so the Holy Father gave him a special blessing. Father Révérony looked suspiciously at Thérèse, tall and pale under her black mantilla. "It is absolutely forbidden to speak to the Holy Father!" he said suddenly and loudly.

Thérèse shot a glance of panic at Céline. If she obeyed, it would mean the end of all the hopes that had kept her spirits up on the long journey. "Speak!" whispered Céline, and the next moment Thérèse found herself kneeling at the Holy Father's feet. She kissed his foot, as pilgrims used to do to show reverence for Christ, whom he represented.

Then, seizing the hand he held out to her, she looked up at him through her tears.

"Holy Father," she said urgently, "I want to ask you a great favor." He bent his head till it almost touched hers, and his black eyes seemed to see right into her soul.

"Holy Father, in honor of your jubilee, let me enter Carmel at fifteen." But her voice shook.

The Pope turned to Father Révérony. "I don't quite understand," he said questioningly.

Father Révérony was furious. Supposing the Pope gave permission over the Bishop's head? "Holy Father," he said hastily, "this is a child who wants to enter Carmel. The Superiors are already going into the matter."

The Pope looked at Thérèse and saw the longing in her eyes as she looked up at him, but he would not overrule the Bishop. "Very well, my child," he said kindly, "do what the Superiors decide."

Thérèse was desperate. She forgot where she was; she cared nothing for all the people watching. She clasped her hands on the Pope's knees and tried once more. "Holy Father, if you say 'yes,' everyone else will be willing."

But the Pope works with the other Bishops, not against them. He did not refuse her, but he could not promise anything. "Well," he said, "you will enter if it is God's will." That, after all, was the important thing; in Carmel or out of it, she must do God's will. But to Thérèse it seemed the end of her hopes. She knelt on at his feet, ready to plead again. But other people were waiting, and when she did not get up, two of the guards lifted her and led her away. The Holy Father turned to look after her and lifted his hand in blessing.

11. *Good-bye*

THERESE left the Vatican in tears, and this time she did not even try to stop them. Nothing seemed any use. And, of course, it was still pouring. In her room at the hotel, her tears gradually stopped; she had time to think things over. At last she saw that the Holy Father had been right: ". . . if it is God's will." She had done all she could, and yet Jesus seemed not to care, like a child throwing a toy into a corner. Very well, she would be a little toy—content to be forgotten. "God has given me courage to bear this trial," she wrote that night to her favorite sister, "but it is very great. But, Pauline, I am the little plaything of the Child Jesus, and if he wants to break his toy he is very welcome. I cannot write any more to you, for Father may come and ask to see what I have written, and that would be impossible, for he would suffer too greatly if he found out how much I am suffering."

But Monsieur Martin was no fool. He did not need to

read her letter to know what his daughter was going through.

The next day, Thérèse and Céline went with the rest of the pilgrims to Naples and Pompeii, where Thérèse felt that the ruins left by the eruption of Vesuvius fitted in very well with the ruin of her hopes. She would have liked to wander about by herself and give way to gloomy thoughts about earthly hopes and riches, but the brisk guides were always there to hurry them on. She hated the huge luxury hotel in Naples where they stayed, and though she thought the bay very lovely, she was too depressed to be really interested. To crown it all, the carriage in which they had been sight-seeing up to the beautiful convent of San Martino was nearly overturned on the way back when the horses bolted. They got back safely, but badly shaken, and Thérèse was only too thankful to reach Rome next day, where the pilgrimage was getting ready for the return journey to France. They could not leave too soon for Thérèse, but she was a little comforted by something her father told her, for he had not gone to Naples but stayed in Rome and visited the head of St. Joseph's College, Brother Simeon.

Monsieur Martin told Brother Simeon the whole story of Thérèse's vocation and asked for his help, because he knew quite a lot of important people at the Vatican.

Brother Simeon was very much interested and astonished when he heard her story. "A thing like that would never happen in Italy!" he exclaimed. "I shall be very glad to do what I can for her."

Just then another visitor was shown in—Father Révérony. He looked a bit sheepish when he saw who was there and seemed to be feeling sorry for what he had done the day before, especially when Monsieur Martin reminded him that he had promised to be helpful. Like everyone else who got to know Thérèse, Father Révérony found himself being influenced by the sheer energy of her own conviction. Thérèse believed so absolutely in her vocation that other people found themselves believing, too. Father Révérony began to feel that he might have been wrong, and being a good-natured man, he was willing to admit it. "I'll be there for her clothing," he said, smiling. "I shall invite myself to it!"

They were to visit Assisi on the way home, and at one of the first stops on the way there, one of the priests organizing the pilgrimage—the one who had named their compartment—came to the door of the carriage where Céline and Thérèse were alone, for the others had gone to get a snack at the station. He smiled at Thérèse. "How is our little Carmelite getting on?" he said. Thérèse did not know where to look. She had tried so hard to look cheerful, she had been sure that only the people who stood quite near had heard her speak to the Pope. Now it seemed that the whole pilgrimage knew! Indeed, many people looked kindly at her and seemed to sympathize, but she was thankful that at least no one tried to talk to her about it.

At Assisi they saw the Portiuncula, the little church where the first "Little Brothers" of St. Francis lived, and the monastery of St. Damian, where St. Clare came after she had run away from her rich home to be a nun and to serve God by praying for the work of her friend Francis. On the way back, Thérèse discovered she had lost the buckle of her belt in the monastery. By the time she had found it and put it on again, it was late; and when she got to the door, all the carriages but one had left for the station. The last carriage was Father Révérony's. If she walked, she would miss the train; she could not catch up with the others—they were far ahead. There was only one thing to do: she must ask for a seat in his carriage. Trying to look carefree, but stiff with embarrassment, she went up and explained what had happened. The carriage was already full, but one person kindly gave her his seat and went to sit beside the driver, so Thérèse found herself, to her horror, in the best seat and right opposite the man who had ruined all her plans.

She felt like a squirrel caught in a trap. But Father Révérony felt differently about her now, and when he saw, in spite of all her efforts, how frightened and uncomfortable she was, he was really sorry for what he had done and did his best to cheer her up. He talked to her about Carmel. "I will leave nothing undone that can help you to enter at fifteen," he assured her. It was a much happier Thérèse who got into the train for Florence.

Florence is one of the loveliest cities in Italy, between its hills of olive groves, with the river flowing through it, spanned by world-famous bridges. The walls of the churches are brilliant with frescoes, and people from every country come to see the pictures of the great Florentine painters in the Uffizi Gallery. Most of the pilgrims went there, but Thérèse had only one idea in her head: she rushed off to the Carmelite convent, where she knelt before the tomb of St. Mary Magdalen de Pazzi, who had been a nun there, and begged her prayers.

Thérèse wanted to get home. They passed through Pisa and Genoa; she just fidgeted to get on. She was glad to see the lovely coast of the Italian Riviera flashing past the train windows, the sea so close that on a stormy day the waves dashed almost up to the tracks. At night the bright lights of the sea ports showed like stars, but she was glad to see them vanish behind her as the train rushed on. Two more short stops, then they reached Paris on December 2 and went on to Lisieux. There was *Les Buissonnets,* the familiar garden, her little room. The great pilgrimage was over.

They were home again. Now what? Monsieur Martin hopefully suggested another pilgrimage—this time to the Holy Land. For a moment, Thérèse caught her breath in excitement at the idea of seeing the very places where her Lord had walked and taught, eaten and slept and prayed, suffered and died and risen to glory. But what would be the use now? It was in Carmel that she wanted to seek her love, not across the sea. She wanted to be a prisoner as soon as possible, to win the freedom of God for other people.

She was still hoping to be allowed to enter on Christmas Day. After the Martins' return, they went to Carmel to visit Marie and Pauline and tell them all about their adventures and to ask for advice.

Pauline knew at once what to do. "You must write to the Bishop," she said, "and remind him that he promised you a written answer. You have not had one yet. Write and ask him if you can enter at Christmas."

Thérèse went home and began her letter. It took her a long time, and when she had finished she took it to Monsieur Guérin to see what he thought of it. He thought it too simple and helped her to rewrite it, making it more formal and respectful. She posted the letter and began counting the days. The hours, the weeks dragged by; but no answer came. Every day she went to the post office after Mass. What was the matter? Was the Bishop offended? Why didn't he write? She wrote to Father Révérony, begging him to do all he could. Still no answer.

Christmas came without any letter; the day was less cheerful than usual, though they all tried hard to be as gay as in other years. On their visit to Carmel, the nuns sang to them a song that Pauline had written. In her room at home, Thérèse found a tiny ship in which lay a model of the Holy Child, asleep, holding a little ball in his hand—the little ball that Thérèse had said was herself, the plaything of the Child Jesus.

As they sat by the fire watching the big yule log, Monsieur Martin must have thought of next Christmas, when there would be no Thérèse to lean against his knee and listen to his songs and stories. But through all those long days and weeks of waiting, he never said a word of his own sorrow.

On New Year's Day came a letter at last, from Mother Marie Gonzaga. The Bishop, she said, had written directly

*Zélie and Louis Martin,
Thérèse's parents*

Three-year-old Thérèse, July 1876

Thérèse's playthings

The Martins' home, Les Buissonnets, *at Lisieux*

Fifteen-year-old Thérèse, about to enter Carmel, April 1888

Thérèse in her novice's robes, January 1889

The Martin sisters and Mother Marie Gonzaga: Céline and Pauline (standing); Mother Marie, Marie, and Thérèse (seated)

Thérèse, aged twenty-two, as Joan of Arc in a convent play

The convent, inside the cloister

The community laundry

The community at recreation

*A family group: Marie Guérin (seated in front); Pauline
and Thérèse (second row); Marie and Céline (third row)*

Thérèse as sacristan with her sisters and cousin

*Thérèse and her novices with Mother Marie Gonzaga and
Sister Agnes (Pauline)*

Thérèse Martin, Sister Thérèse of the Child Jesus and of the Holy Face, shortly before her death, June 1897

to her, saying that he would allow Thérèse to enter at once. Thérèse's spirits soared, but she read on. Mother Marie had decided that, all the same, she should not enter until after Lent. She thought it would not be a good idea for so young a girl to begin her religious life with the extra hardships and penances of a Carmelite Lent. She also hoped that the delay would smooth the ruffled pride of Father Delatröette, who was still against the whole plan, but this Thérèse found out afterward. Now she knew only that she must wait three months. Three months! It seemed like years to her then. How could she bear it? For a moment, she rebelled—she might as well enjoy those three months, since this waiting was forced on her. It was her last chance—why not have a little fun while she could, relax a bit? She shook herself and pushed that idea firmly away. If she had to wait three months, she must see to it that she spent the time preparing as well as she could for her life in Carmel. She would try more than ever to lead a life of sacrifice.

She tried never to miss a chance of checking her self-will, never to answer back. She found small things to do quietly for other people. She spent a lot of time with her father, who did everything he could to please her during these last weeks.

She also went to pay a farewell visit to the abbey to tell the nuns the news and thank them for all they had done. She arrived during a drawing lesson. Mother Saint Léon, the drawing mistress, looked up. "Why, Thérèse," she said, "you have put up your hair!"

"Yes, Madame," she answered, and after a moment the nun went to speak to her outside, for she did not want the other girls to hear.

The girls whispered curiously to one another, watching the two of them as they talked in the passage and wondering what it was all about. Thérèse Martin had always been an odd girl. When Mother Saint Léon came back she was silent and seemed to be thinking over something that surprised her.

The ninth of April, 1888, was the day chosen. The evening before, Monsieur and Madame Guérin, with Jeanne and Marie, came to supper at *Les Buissonnets*. They all tried to be cheerful on this last evening together, but no one really felt very gay. Léonie, who had sadly left the novitiate of the Poor Clare convent because her health could not stand the strict life, had warned Thérèse what it might be like. She watched her sister across the table, so young and so brave, and was generous enough to pray that Thérèse would not have to suffer as she herself had suffered. Céline watched her, too, unselfish Céline who had put off her own hope of being a nun to let Thérèse go first. She had to stay at home and look after their father, perhaps for many, many years. But she was happy for her sister, and her own sacrifice was made in silence. And their father, at the head of the table, knew this was the last time she would sit beside him. He was no longer strong, but he might live for years in greater and greater weakness, without her pretty face to cheer him, the gay sound of her voice to lighten the long days. He smiled at her affectionately and turned to make conversation with his sister-in-law.

Thérèse was up early next morning, and when she was dressed she went around the house and garden saying goodbye to each familiar thing. She turned out the trinkets in her jewel case, the little crosses, her earrings, the butterfly brooch, the medal of the Roman pilgrimage on its blue ribbon. She fingered the mantilla she had worn when she knelt before the Holy Father. She wandered through the house touching the furniture she had known for so long, the big round dining-room table with the straight-backed chairs around it, the carved sideboard, the lamp which was lit for the family gatherings in the evening. Here was the hearth where the Christmas shoes were laid out and the yule log burned. Out in the garden she walked once more past the bench where she had told her father of her vocation. Here were the little garden patch that had been her very own and the tiny crib arranged in a hollow of the wall. Outside that washhouse she had seen the strange vision of her father, bent and with his face veiled. She went indoors and, before they left, knelt for the last time before the statue of Our Lady, remembering her smile, asking now for strength and courage like hers.

The three girls and their father walked to Mass together. In the public chapel of Carmel, they received communion side by side, and Thérèse could hear all around her the sound of stifled sobs. They walked in procession to the cloister door, Thérèse in front, dry-eyed and pale, her heart hammering in her chest until she wondered whether she were going to die. They kissed her in turn, then she knelt down for her father's blessing. He wept, but Thérèse, in an agony of sorrow, did not cry at all. She turned her back on them, and Monsieur Martin watched the cloister door slowly close behind his "little queen."

12. A New Life

J UST IN CASE Thérèse should feel glad to have reached her goal at last, Canon Delatröette received her with words that were like a bucket of cold water. "Well, Reverend Mother," said he loudly, while the enclosure door was not yet shut and her father could hear every word, "you can now sing your 'Te Deum.' As the Bishop's delegate, I present to you this child of fifteen years, whose entry you have wanted so much. I trust she will not disappoint your hopes, but if she does, may I remind you that it will be entirely your own fault."

There was an uncomfortable silence for a moment, but the nuns hurried to put things right, and Thérèse found herself being affectionately kissed by each in turn, her own sisters among them. They all went to the choir, where she knelt at the feet of Mother Geneviève, the foundress. Then she was taken to see all the rooms of the convent and finally to her cell, where she was left for a little while.

The nuns who had never known Thérèse were astonished. They had expected a child, possibly a spoiled child, but what they saw when she came through the cloister door was a tall young woman, her face grave in spite of its still childish roundness, with a firm line to her mouth and chin that showed the self-control and courage gained by years of self-discipline.

Thérèse, left alone, had time to calm down after what she had just been through and to look around her. She was glad to be there and very peaceful. She knew quite well that her life would be hard, but that was what she wanted. Looking around her cell, everything pleased her: the bare whitewashed walls, the hard bed with its straw mattress, the plain little stool and worktable, the hourglass, the water jug and lamp, and the plain cross on the wall. It was all perfect. This was really at last the desert place for which she had longed. "I am here forever now," she kept on saying to herself. "I am here forever!"

She put on the dress of a postulant, which she had to wear for at least six months—until she was clothed with the Carmelite habit as a novice. She wore a plain blue ankle-length woollen dress that she had brought with her and put on a little black cape like the one she had worn at school, then she coiled up her shining hair under a tight bonnet of coarse black net. The mistress of novices, Mother Marie of the Angels, took her to the Novitiate (the part of the convent set aside for the postulants and novices) and introduced her to the novices. Mother Marie had known her since she was nine, when she used to come to the parlor to see her sister Pauline and later Marie, too. She was very fond of the new postulant and already admired her for her sweetness and courage.

Thérèse threw herself into her new life with enthusiasm. In the morning she was awakened at five o'clock by the din of a loud clapper of iron on hard wood. She jumped up from her hard bed, washed hastily in the cold water, and scrambled into her clothes. All the community went in silence to the chapel for an hour's silent prayer, then they recited the Office of Prime, the first part of the divine office for the morning. Next came Mass and holy communion, and after that they went to breakfast, a piece of bread and a mug of coffee, eaten standing up. Between the hours for the divine office and the hours set aside for silent prayer, each nun had her special work to do. Thérèse's first job was to help Mother Marie of the Angels, the novice mistress, in the linen room. There, the clothes for the community were made and mended, and she learned to patch and patch and darn and darn, until the linen and wool were so worn that she could see her own fingers through them as she worked. Only when a garment practically fell to pieces could it be replaced and used up as dusters or bandages, for not even rags must be wasted in a convent vowed to poverty. Thérèse was bad at sewing—her sisters had always done it for the "little queen" at home—so she got plenty of scoldings for her bad, slow work from other Sisters. Besides this work, she had a dormitory and a staircase to sweep. Before the meal at midday, there was a visit to the chapel, then they went in procession to the refectory, where they sang grace. When the Prioress gave the word, they all sat down and ate in silence while one of the nuns read aloud from some pious book. The food was very plain, they never ate meat, and during Lent there were no fish, cheese, or eggs either.

Thérèse ate what was given her without fuss, and as she never showed what she liked or didn't like, she was often given the scraps and leftovers that no one else wanted. She did not tell her father this when she wrote home. "I've never had so much to eat as I've had since I came to Carmel!" she told him in one letter. Certainly he did his best to see that she did, for huge parcels of vegetables and fish arrived from him.

"You cannot imagine how much pleasure your carp, your *monster* carp, has given us—dinner was half an hour late! Sister Marie of the Sacred Heart made the sauce. It was delicious, just like *worldly* cooking." What she did not tell him was that a lot of the food gave her indigestion, and as Mother Marie of the Angels had told her always to report it, poor Thérèse had to go to her nearly every day.

The trouble was that kind Mother Marie had forgotten all about her order, and Thérèse's continued complaints made her think the girl was ill. Off went Mother Marie to the Prioress to get some medicine, and Mother Marie Gonzaga, who did not like sick people, was annoyed. "If she cannot keep quiet about her aches and pains, she's no business here!" she said crossly. In terror of being sent away, Thérèse went on obediently reporting her indigestion, though she would rather have had ten stomach-aches, until at last the novice mistress remembered her order and said she need not do so any more.

Twice a day, after dinner and supper, there was recreation—a time for talking in the community room—but most of their spare moments the nuns spent, each in her own cell, working or praying. There was an hour's free time after the midday recreation, then more work until Vespers, in the middle of the afternoon. After this there was time for reading, and the novices and postulants had a special talk from the novice mistress about the religious life and the Carmelite Order. Then came another two hours' work and an hour of silent prayer in the choir. Supper was a very small meal, and after the last recreation they said Compline. An hour of free time followed before they sang the night Office, Matins. and Lauds for the next day. Then someone read aloud a short piece from a pious book, and they went to bed.

During the day no one spoke except when she had to, and every evening after Compline was over there began the Great Silence, which lasted until after Mass next morning. During this time the silence might be broken only for a very serious reason. Thérèse tried to make every moment of her new life an act of love for her Lord. She had known it would be hard; just how hard she had not perhaps guessed, for she had more to suffer than the ordinary hardships and penances of the Rule. Almost from the first day, God seemed far off, and she was left to struggle, uncomforted, with difficulties which seemed at times quite pointless. But she clung to the Lord who hid himself. He had brought her here to give up everything to his service. Very well, she would do just that, even to giving up cheerfully the comfort of his daily help. She wrote to Céline about it: "It is hard to begin the day's work when Jesus hides himself from one's love. What has become of that kind Friend? If he sees our misery and the heavy weight we have to carry, why doesn't he come and encourage us? But don't be afraid—he is there, just beside you. He is watching. He begs these trials and tears from us because he wants them for souls, our own and other people's." And Thérèse went off to her work. To an outsider her life might have seemed dreary, painful, useless, but to her every detail was a joy, because every small action was an act of love.

She swept the cloister, doing her best and finding it hard, for she had never done much housework at home. Down the cloister came the impressive figure of Mother Marie Gonzaga, her eyes, over the top of her glasses, searching every cranny. She came up behind Thérèse, who was bent over her broom, and pointed an accusing finger at a cobweb dangling in a dim corner. "It's easy to see our cloisters are swept by a child of fifteen," she said loudly, while other nuns working near turned their heads curiously. "It's disgraceful! Go and sweep away that cobweb, and be more careful in future!" She swept on, while Thérèse knelt, her eyes on the ground, blushing scarlet. She thanked God as she knelt there, broom in hand, for this humiliation that made her more like her Master. If this was her happiness, she could never have too much of it—and she got plenty.

Mother Marie of the Angels, who believed in fresh air, sent her every afternoon at half-past four to weed the garden. Thérèse went obediently, but with a sinking feeling inside, trying not to look over her shoulder. Sure enough as she moved down the garden with her little basket, she heard behind her the familiar dreaded footsteps and the loud, harsh voice: "Really, this child does absolutely nothing! What's the use of a postulant who has to be sent for a walk every afternoon?"

Mother Marie Gonzaga was a strange woman. She had a sharp tongue and a quick temper, and some of the novices were afraid of her. Even the older nuns found her difficult to get on with. Neither had she any sympathy for the weak or ill. "Nowadays people have illnesses that no one even heard of before—it's foolish to nurse them," she said sharply.

She was very intelligent and good at organizing, but she was jealous and could not bear anyone else to seem more important than she. As Prioress she could often be wise and understanding, but when she was not in office she was a troublemaker. And since she came from an aristocratic family, she was inclined to look down on nuns from more humble homes and expect special privileges—even things that were not allowed by the Rule of the Order. There was a great deal that was wrong in the Carmel of Lisieux, as Thérèse discovered, and much of it could be traced to Mother Marie Gonzaga. But with all her faults, she could be generous, and she really loved Thérèse, in her twisted way. But her affection did not prevent her from using her sharp tongue on the new postulant, for—unconsciously interpreting Thérèse's character in the light of her own—she felt sure that the distinction of having entered so young must have made Thérèse conceited and in need of snubs to keep her humble.

No wonder Thérèse did not look forward to the time she spent with the Prioress, when she was supposed to get spiritual help and advice. Mother Marie spent the whole hour scolding her, about her slowness, her inefficiency in her jobs, and a dozen other things. Coming out from this long ordeal, Thérèse would stand in the passage for a moment to pull herself together. She tried to be glad because God was leading her the hard way—his own way. Suppose they had made a pet of her because she was so young. She might easily have drifted into the sort of self-indulgent friendships she had learned to distrust. She went to her cell and took out her sewing, and when the time came in which she was free to do as she liked, instead of trying to find comfort in prayer, as she wanted to do, she bent her head steadily over her work. Mother Prioress had said she was slow and not thorough in her work; surely she would like her to go on with it. But there was no one in the bare little cell to notice or tell the Prioress. Only God saw.

And Thérèse would have been very surprised if she could have seen a letter that her uncle and aunt got at this time. "I would never have believed," wrote the Prioress, who had just been scolding Thérèse, "that a girl of fifteen could be so grown up and sensible."

The novice mistress was an altogether different kind of woman. She was as kind as could be, but rather a bore. Thérèse had to spend most of the day with her, and Mother Marie of the Angels talked to her about her soul until Thérèse squirmed with embarrassment—but not outwardly, for she forced herself to listen and to be grateful for her mistress's kind intention. What was more, she was expected to talk to her mistress about herself, and Thérèse found this terribly difficult, so she came to hate these hours with the kind novice mistress and almost to long for Mother Gonzaga's stern speeches. What should she say? Very unwillingly, she told the novice mistress about the pain she felt at the way the Prioress treated her, but explained hurriedly that, of course, she did not mind—it was all for her good—and she gave her mistress the smile that all the nuns were getting to know so well. Mother Marie of the Angels was worried by this confession, and she tried to make up for the Prioress's strictness by making Thérèse sleep on in the morning sometimes. This only made matters worse, for when she was made to do this for a whole fortnight, the Prioress noticed and thought Thérèse was being lazy.

At the end of May, Marie made her vows, and Thérèse, the youngest of the community, put on her head the wreath of white roses. It was a happy day for the three sisters. There were not many family days for them, for Thérèse felt that it would be wrong for her to look for comfort in the company of her sisters when the strictness of the Prioress or the cattiness of some other nuns made her unhappy. She thought that ordinary family affection must be sacrificed; instead, she must try to love her sisters as God loved them. At recreation, she sat next to whoever happened to be near—unless someone seemed to be left alone, then she filled the gap. Marie was told to look after her at first, until she got used to the ways of the convent, and to show her how to mark her choir book so as to find the right places for divine office. Thérèse, worried that they should be talking so much over it instead of keeping the silence, ventured to say that she could manage by herself. Marie was a little hurt by this, and Thérèse was sad at having to hurt her. But afterward Marie and Pauline both realized that Thérèse was not ungrateful or selfish. She was simply trying very hard to discover the deepest kind of love, which is something much greater than the pleasure we get from the company of people we love—though that is part of it, too—and at first Thérèse went too far in her strictness, as young and enthusiastic people often do.

In the world outside, life went on, and most of the people who had known Thérèse no longer thought of her, except as a pleasant memory. At the abbey, girls who had done their lessons with her were still schoolgirls, though most of them were in their final year. Sometimes, that summer, they wondered about Thérèse. They had never got on with her very well at school—she was too quiet, too pious, too reserved —but a girl who went into the strict Carmelite convent at fifteen was queer enough to make them inquisitive. Would she have changed? What would she look like? What sort of life did she lead? Finally, a group of them went to Mother Sainte Placide and asked whether they might go and see her, and it was arranged during the Whitsun holiday.

The convent parlor was dreary and empty, just a few stiff chairs, one or two very dull pictures, and the big double grille of crisscrossed iron bars, one behind the other. The grille nearest to themselves had knobs sticking out of it. They felt it was like a prison. Then the shutters on the other side opened, and there was Thérèse in her shapeless postulant's dress, with the black cape and bonnet. Although she looked so odd, the girls felt comfortable with her at once. She asked about the school and the nuns, and soon they were talking quite easily. She spoke a little—only a little—of her life in the convent and made them laugh over a pair of shoes she wore that squeaked. All the Sisters knew who was coming, just by the noise, she said. By the time the half hour was over and Thérèse had closed the shutters, they had quite decided to come again. On the way back, some of them wondered why they had not taken more notice of her before.

There were other times when Céline and Léonie came to the parlor to see their sisters in the convent. Sometimes Thérèse was the only one to see them, and she longed to talk for hours and hours to her dear Céline—letters were so little use after the long talks they used to have. But the sand in the hourglass that measured the time for the visit ran steadily through, and as the last grains fell, Thérèse got up, closed the shutters, and went back to her work.

All the while she could not find in herself any feelings of love for God. She even began to have scruples again—to

worry over tiny things. Could it be her own fault, this darkness in which God hid himself? She tried hard to tell her
novice mistress about it but found it almost impossible to
explain, and kind Mother Marie just made long speeches of
good advice and encouragement as the two worked together,
patching, darning, and making habits, until Thérèse longed
to run from the room. Instead, she sat still at her stitching
and smiled and tried to listen.

Then one day Father Pichon, a Jesuit priest, came to the
convent to give a retreat—a few days of extra sermons and
prayers, when all but essential work was excused. Thérèse
knew about him, for he had often helped her older sisters,
and she had written to him herself before she entered. He
was interested in her and expected to find a sweet and pious
little girl, led by God along easy paths. When Thérèse came
to talk to him in the convent parlor, she needed help badly,
but she found it, as usual, dreadfully difficult to´ explain
what was the matter. Father Pichon understood without being told that she was no longer a child, but a young woman
whom God was leading by a road of suffering. But her progress in love was being blocked by worries over childish faults,
and after she had made a general confession of her whole
life to him, he tried to help her to get rid of this worry. "Before God, Our Lady, the angels, and all the saints, I declare
that you have never committed a serious sin. Thank God for
giving you such a great grace without any merit on your
part."

She felt that it was a message from God and never worried
over her sins any more. But the darkness did not lift, and
since Father Pichon went to Canada soon afterward, Thérèse was left alone again, very alone, for no one else knew
what she was suffering. Yet her happiness in serving God
showed in her face, always serene, often gay. She wrote cheerful, affectionate letters to her aunts and cousins, and she did
not admit even to Céline all that she was suffering, for to

her the glory of her life was much more important than the pain. Above all, she tried to cheer up her father, for he missed her dreadfully. He consoled himself by loading the convent with more and more presents of fish that he caught himself and baskets of fruit. "Baby Jesus's postman," Thérèse called him in her letters. She reminded him often of the amusing things they had done on their great journey— the Vatican guide who pronounced long words all wrong, the time they pretended to "trail" some acquaintances as if they had been detectives.

Then he had another stroke and was very ill. Thérèse longed to be with him, but she made her pain and anxiety for him another act of love for God and wrote her father letters full of bits of news and loving little jokes. He got a little better and again sent enormous baskets of fruit and vegetables. "What huge onions!" she wrote. "It did me good to see them!" But much more exciting was the lace he sent, which would trim the dress that was being made for her clothing day, still so far off. It was *point d'Alençon*, the kind of lace her mother had made. When a girl is going to receive the habit of a novice, she is dressed first of all in a wedding dress. It is a sign that she is to be dedicated to Christ, who, St. Paul says, loves the Church, the assembly of God's people, as the bridegroom loves the bride. These "brides of Christ" are to show by their whole lives that the mystery of human life is a mystery of love, and the bridal finery is a reminder of this. And young nuns-to-be naturally want their wedding dresses to be every bit as gorgeous as those of their friends who are getting married. So thought Thérèse as she admired the lace that her father had sent. "It's much too beautiful for your 'queen,' but nothing is too good for the Divine Husband to whom you have given her, so I shall love to wear it," she wrote to him. Her gaiety was not a pretense. Her worry and real pain were happiness to her, because they brought her close to love, and that was the greatest possible happiness.

As the year drew to a close, the open cloisters and unheated rooms of the Carmel filled with autumn mist, and the stones were cold to touch. Thérèse was only a postulant still, and as she was so young, she was well cared for. Sister Agnes told her she must have a pair of furry slippers, so she wrote to Marie Guérin to ask for some. "Jeanne can try them on for me," she wrote. "Her feet are exactly the same size as mine.

"You cannot imagine how well looked after I am in Carmel," she added. "I am forever having to eat and warm my feet." She did not add that the extra food gave her indigestion and that the only place for warming oneself was at a tiny fire in the recreation room, where the nuns could go only occasionally.

Whatever cosseting Thérèse got because she was so young would soon have to stop. The day was coming at last when she would be clothed with the Carmelite habit and share fully in the life of the community. Canon Delatröette had delayed things as long as he could, still sure that she was too young, but in the end he had to give in. The date was fixed for January 9.

13. *The* *Bride*

A WEEK before the clothing, Madame Guérin sent both a bunch and a wreath of artificial lilies, and Thérèse wrote to thank her for them. The nuns were busy sewing her dress of white velvet with the wonderful lace her father had sent and yards of soft swansdown.

All over the convent there was a bustle of preparation for the great day, and Monsieur Martin, who was a little better, sent one huge parcel after another for the occasion.

The ceremony had to be put off for one day because the Bishop could not come on the ninth.

Three days before her clothing, Thérèse went into retreat. This meant that she was excused from work and spent extra time each day with the Prioress and mistress of novices for help and advice. She did not speak to any of the other nuns during this time, but Mother Marie Gonzaga gave her special permission to write notes to her two sisters in the convent. In these notes she told them what no one else could have guessed—that her "dryness" was worse than ever, that she had no feeling of love or devotion to God. But she was glad, she said, because if God had allowed her any feeling of ordinary happiness, she might have clung to that and not to him alone. It was better to be without it, so that her offering might be all for him.

The morning of January 10 was unusually warm for the time of the year, and Thérèse was a little disappointed because she had hoped very much that it would snow. She had always loved the snow, as white as the white dress she put on that morning. The bodice fitted her closely from her neck to below her waist, and from the hips fell rich folds ornamented with lace and swansdown and gathered into a small bustle and a sweeping train at the back. Her hair, freed from the ugly black bonnet, fell down her back in curls that had been brushed until they gleamed, and over it went the fine soft net, held in place by the wreath of lilies her aunt had sent.

Quietly, but glowing with real happiness, Thérèse walked through the cloister, to the door of the enclosure—the door through which she had passed with such agony nine months before. Now it opened again, and as she stepped out, her father came forward to meet her.

It was a shock to see him. He looked so old, so ill, and yet so happy at seeing her. He had given everything he had to God, and he had this last day of perfect happiness. How beautiful she looked to him standing in the doorway. "Here is my little queen," he said, and kissed her. Then he gave her his arm, though he was barely strong enough, and together they went slowly into the chapel. Behind them came Céline and Léonie, the Guérins, and other relations and friends, filing two by two into their places. Then the Mass began, and as the Bishop of Bayeux moved slowly from side to side and the Holy Sacrifice was offered, Thérèse knelt alone, right in front. On her right was the dark arched grille and the black curtain which separated the public from where her Sisters were praying for her. After Mass everyone went back to the enclosure door in procession, and Thérèse was able to kiss her father and relatives for the last time.

The Bishop gave her his blessing as she knelt before him, then she turned away from them all and passed once more through the door, a lighted candle in her hand. The Bishop went back to the chapel.

Inside the convent, Thérèse was met by all the nuns carrying lighted candles, and as they passed along the cloister, she looked up at the statue of the Child Jesus smiling down on her from among the pink candles and the flowers she had arranged for him herself. Turning away, something caught her eye, and she stared amazed through the arches at the open quadrangle, for the square space was covered with a thin icing of snow. She had wanted snow. Perhaps it was silly and rather babyish to care so much, but just because she knew her wish for snow was slightly childish, it seemed to her, all the more, a touching sign that God cared for her, cared even for her foolish whim. The powdering of snow, as white as her wedding dress, was like a little unexpected present from someone one loves.

In the chapel, the big curtain that usually covered the grille dividing the nuns' choir from the part reserved for the congregation was drawn back. Everyone could see into the choir, and the Bishop sat waiting beside the grille.

Once again Thérèse's family saw her coming, shining in white among the black-veiled nuns, but this time the thick crisscrossing of iron was between them and her.

As she knelt before him behind the bars, the Bishop spoke to her as the voice of the Church. "What do you ask?" he began solemnly.

"The mercy of God, the poverty of the Order, and the company of the Sisters," answered Thérèse in her clear voice.

"Is it of your own free will and of your own accord that you wish to take the religious habit?"

"Yes."

"Do you wish to enter this Order for the sole love of Our Lord?"

"Yes," she said, "by the grace of God and with the prayers of the Sisters."

She got up from her knees and was led away from the choir, while the nuns sang a Psalm, and through the grille the Bishop blessed the cloak and scapular and the belt laid out on a stool.

In one of the rooms of the convent, two of the nuns helped Thérèse to change. Off came the lovely white dress, the lilies, the floating veil. The long hair she had brushed so carefully that morning was cut, and her head suddenly felt oddly light as the curls fell in a shining pile at her feet.

They put on her the brown Carmelite habit and the rope-soled sandals; the "toque" or wimple of coarse linen went over her cropped head, and over that the novice's white veil.

When, once more, her father and sisters saw her coming up the choir, she was no longer a proud, shining swan, but a humble little brown sparrow.

While she stood there like a penitent in sackcloth, two nuns put the belt on her while the Bishop blessed her, saying, "When thou wast younger, thou didst gird thyself and walked whither thou wouldst; but when thou shalt grow old, another shall gird thee. In the name of the Father and of the Son and of the Holy Ghost."

Then over her head went the brown scapular, and they arranged it on her shoulders, like the straps of a load that was heavy to carry. "Receive the sweet yoke of Christ and his light burden," the Bishop read from his book, and went on: "They that follow the Lamb without stain shall walk with him in white; therefore let your garment be ever white, as a sign of inward purity."

As he read, the nuns hung around her brown shoulders the sweeping choir cloak of white wool, so that she shone once more from head to foot. But this time it was the white of a nun among other nuns. Mother Marie Gonzaga led her back to the middle of the choir, and there, on a plain brown carpet in the middle, she lay down on her face, her arms stretched out like the arms of Christ on the cross. And all around her were ferns and hothouse plants, for the flowers they wanted were hard to get in January. The nuns, like everyone else at that time, liked to have as many flowers and plants as possible, and friends had been very generous on this occasion.

"Te Deum Laudamus . . ." The Bishop suddenly began to intone the Church's great song of thanksgiving, praise, and triumph.

But a priest hurried up to him. "The Te Deum is sung only at professions, Monseigneur," came the agitated whisper in his ear. Kindly but firmly the Bishop of Bayeux waved him away and went on singing. He knew it was a great day.

When the Te Deum and some prayers were finished, the Prioress sprinkled Thérèse with holy water. Then, touching her lightly as a signal to rise, she led her to the altar in the choir. Thérèse kissed it and then passed down the choir from one nun to another, to be kissed by each in turn, for now she was no longer an outsider but a new Sister, one of the family. Among the welcoming faces were those of her own sisters, and they greeted her sedately like the rest, but in their smiles they showed her how happy they were to have her with them.

Then it was all over, and they left the choir. The black curtain was drawn across the grille, shutting out the world.

Afterward Thérèse saw her father for a few minutes in the parlor, and he was able to look at her carefully in her Carmelite clothes. He was very happy.

Unlike Monsieur Martin, who could see her only through the double grille of the parlor, the Bishop was allowed inside the enclosure, with several priests who had come with him. To him Thérèse seemed little more than a child, and he made a great fuss of her, talking about the famous visit to Bayeux and the pilgrimage to Rome. "Do you remember how you put up your hair when you visited me?" he asked, smiling, and for a moment he took her head in his hands, the head that now wore a veil over her hair, cut short like a boy's.

After all the visitors had gone, they had a party in the convent. There were special dishes at dinner and wine to drink, and afterward they crowded around and lit the fuse of a huge artificial pumpkin that Monsieur Martin had sent. Everyone waited breathlessly, then suddenly there was a loud bang, and the room was filled with candies flying in all directions.

When Thérèse went to her cell that night, carrying the little lamp that her cousin Marie had bought for her, it was the end of her great day. For the first time she took off her brown scapular and habit, her white veil and toque and put on the night habit and veil in which all the nuns slept.

She lay down on her straw mattress and pulled over her the poor blankets which did not keep out the cold. She was very happy.

Within a month a heavy blow fell, and all five sisters—in the convent and in the world—were faced with a load of suffering which they were to carry for five years.

14. The Novice

WHEN Thérèse received the habit of a Carmelite nun, she was allowed to take as her name in religion "Thérèse of the Child Jesus," just as she had planned to do when she was nine. But now she added to it another title: "and of the Holy Face."

She loved to think of Jesus as a baby and as a little boy, but now still more she thought of him as he looked when he suffered and died for sinners. She thought of his face streaked with blood from the crown of thorns, bruised and swollen from the soldiers' blows, and covered with dust and sweat from the long uphill road to Calvary. Thinking of this made her want even more to show her love for him by sharing in his sufferings, and it was only a month after the day of her clothing that her wish began to come true.

For the rest of January, Monsieur Martin remained quite well. But at the beginning of February, the disease suddenly came back, and this time it affected his brain so that he forgot who he was and wandered off by himself, sometimes for miles.

Once Céline and Léonie lost him for two days, and he was finally found wandering about the port of Le Havre. Then they realized that it was too dangerous for him to live at home; they could not watch him every minute, and the next time he wandered he might be hurt.

He must go to a mental hospital, where he could be properly looked after.

They had to leave their old home, which they had grown to love so much, and all their favorite corners and bits of furniture. They went to Caen and took their father to the huge asylum there. He was quite clear in his mind then and knew everything that was happening. It was dreadful for him and almost worse for his daughters in the convent and at Caen, who knew what he was going through and could do nothing to help him.

There were plenty of people, too, who made nasty remarks about Monsieur Martin. "That's what comes of being too pious!" said these people to Céline and Léonie, and the same sort of thing was passed on to the three sisters in the convent.

Thérèse remembered how, as a little girl, she had seen that strange vision of her father, bent and old and with a veil over his head. She knew now what it meant: the veil on his head was a sign of the way the disease would destroy his clear mind.

The whole family suffered with their father. Thérèse saw that in this way they were sharing in the suffering of Our Lord, and she thanked God. It hurt more than she could possibly tell anyone, but that was what she had prayed for, and she welcomed it; she even said it was her happiness. This sounds strange and morbid, but Thérèse was not at all morbid. Suffering comes to everyone, whether they like it or not. Sometimes it embitters people and cuts them off from life and love. Thérèse realized that it could, instead, be the way to set free the power of love, as it did in Christ's Passion. What she meant by happiness was not a feeling of pleasure or enjoyment but a deep conviction that she was becoming what a human being is meant to be—a person open to love.

Ordinary life went on, whatever people felt like, and there was a lot to do in the convent. Thérèse's new job was in the refectory. She swept it and wiped the tables and laid them for the next meal. In each place she put a round wooden bowl, a cup, a wooden-handled knife, a fork and spoon. Sometimes they had cider, and then she put out the little jugs for it along the tables, one for two people. (She herself never got any; the jugs were really too small for two people, so Thérèse pretended she did not want hers, and her neighbor drank it all.)

The most difficult part of the refectory work was that Pauline—Sister Agnes—worked there, too. Thérèse wanted so much to talk to her, to comfort her perhaps in their worry about their father, and to hear some kind words from her favorite sister to make up for the scoldings she was always getting from other people. But, of course, they never did talk except to ask for something or when Pauline gave an order; it would have broken the silence without good reason.

Then there was the laundry work, which everyone shared. There was the boiling of the dirty clothes in the boiler or else just the scrubbing of them in cold water, as it is still often done in the country in France. The linen was coarse and heavy, and hands got sore. In the summer and the hot weather, the best place to be was at the rinsing tubs of cold water out of doors. At least it was cool. But Thérèse had not come to Carmel to get the best place. She had come to show God that she loved him, by bearing pain and discomfort for his sake. So she went into the laundry and took her turn cheerfully at lifting and shifting the heavy stuff. It was stifling in there, where one's whole body under the thick habit was soon wet with sweat. Sometimes they sang, so that the work went happily.

Every afternoon the novices had their little talk after Vespers with Mother Marie of the Angels, who tried to teach them to be good Carmelites. Then they were given books from the convent library. There were a lot of heavy books of theology and books about prayer. Thérèse read them, but few seemed to be much help. Some of them, she thought, made prayer seem so complicated that she could never manage to do all the things they said. More and more she found that it was the Bible that helped her most; she read and read it, and every time there seemed to be more things to discover.

The winter came again to Carmel, and this time there were no furry slippers for Thérèse. As 1889 came to an end, she began to look forward with all her heart to the day when she would be allowed to make her vows and belong to God completely (for Carmelites usually spend just a year as novices). But another disappointment was waiting for her. Mother Prioress had to tell her that she was not to be allowed to make her vows yet. Canon Delatröette had interfered again. He still thought her too young and was determined he would at least make her wait as long as possible.

It was a dreadful disappointment. Thérèse was worried about her father and shivering with cold in the damp, drafty convent. God seemed far away, and some of the nuns, who made no secret of their dislike of her, were all too close. The one thing that made it all bearable was the thought that all this was for God, and now she was denied the great comfort of publicly committing herself to him. She could not help feeling, at that moment, angry and almost desperate. It was so unfair. But she had learned by now not to give way to her feelings so easily, and she went to her cell to think the thing out. Why had God denied her this favor? There must be some sense in it.

As she thought, she began to see all kinds of little ways in which she had not been as God would wish. "After all," she said to herself, "a bride does not go to her wedding in her everyday clothes. She spends time and money to make a beautiful wedding dress. Well, then, I will find as many ways of showing my love as I can, and each one will be like a jewel sewn on my dress. Then when it is rich and lovely enough, Jesus will let me take my vows and belong entirely to him, just as a bride belongs to her husband."

There was one thing she could do straight away. There was another girl in the novitiate with Thérèse whom she did not really like. She was stupid and rather bad-tempered, and everyone found her trying. Thérèse realized that liking or not liking someone had nothing to do with the matter; she ought to love all her Sisters, just as God loved them all, whatever they were like. What do people do when they love someone? Talk to them, try to be with them, show they are pleased to see them, thought Thérèse. She set herself to do all that for the moody novice. She sat near her when she could at recreation, she always had a smile for her; and in the end, the difficult novice was so pleased that she came to love Thérèse and to copy her gentleness and kindness.

Mother Marie of the Angels was a very kind woman, but even she was upset when she found a little vase broken because someone had carelessly put it on a window ledge, where the wind had knocked it over. She thought it was Thérèse's fault, so she sent for her and spoke to her severely. Thérèse, in fact, knew nothing about it, but a good nun should not make excuses. She longed to say "It wasn't me," but she shut her mouth firmly and knelt to kiss the ground, as they were all supposed to do when they were reprimanded for a fault. When Mother Marie had finished, Thérèse managed to speak. "I'm very sorry, Mother. I promise I will not be so careless another time," she said in her quiet voice. But how difficult that gentle answer had been to give, only God knew.

All day and every day, as the summer opened out once more and the flowers glowed brilliantly in the convent garden, Thérèse looked for chances to be quietly helpful, to make small sacrifices, to collect more and more "jewels for her dress."

Sometimes after Mass or the Office, one or two of the nuns, in a hurry or from absentmindedness, left their big white choir cloaks lying about instead of folding them. She would wait quietly until the others had gone and fold up the cloaks and put them neatly away.

Then there was an old lay Sister in the convent called Sister St. Peter. She was bent and stiff with rheumatism, so that she could not even walk any more without help; pain and age had made her persnickety, and no one liked having to help her. Thérèse volunteered for the job of helping her to the refectory after prayer every evening, and in the end Sister St. Peter allowed her to try, though she did not like the idea. "You are too young," she grumbled. "You will let me fall." So at the end of prayer, she shook her hourglass as a sign to her helper. Then Thérèse had to pick up her stool and carry it for her, in exactly the way she liked, while Sister St. Peter watched her. Then she had to hold the old nun's belt and support her along the cloister, very, very slowly. The invalid grumbled and complained the whole way. "You are going too fast—I shall break my bones!" she said if she felt Thérèse's hand on her belt to hold her up, but if Thérèse tried to be even gentler she could not feel her hand. "Now you aren't following me, I can't feel your hand, you're letting me go, I shall fall! I was right to say you were too young to look after me!"

One night, a snatch of music from a band in the town floated into the open cloister as they passed along it. Thérèse imagined the cozy homes out there, the gay evening parties, the songs, the pretty dresses. Around her were the damp brick walls of the cloister, under her hand the rough serge of the old nun's habit, and no music but the complaints of the querulous voice. This was better, thought Thérèse, much better. It was good for her to be here.

When they reached the refectory at last, Sister St. Peter had to be arranged just so, her wide sleeves turned back for her, and the job was done. Thérèse might have been thankful to leave the invalid Sister as quickly as possible, but she soon noticed that the old hands were so twisted and stiff that the poor woman could not cut her bread properly. She could only fumble and poke at it. Thérèse leaned over and quietly cut it for her. Then before she left her, she smiled, as if she were especially fond of her. The heart of the old Sister was touched. Gradually she came to love Thérèse in turn.

One evening Thérèse turned to the shelf where the lamps were kept to take her own down, but it was not there. Someone must have taken it by mistake. What a nuisance! It was getting dark, and without it she could not do the reading to which she had been looking forward so much. She felt annoyance rising inside her. She longed to run off and demand her lamp from whoever had taken it, but the time of the Great Silence had begun, so that was impossible.

Disappointed and annoyed, she went back to her cell, but as she went she suddenly thought how silly she was being. Nuns took a vow of poverty, she reflected, and as the Carmelite rule told her, poverty did not just mean doing without extras—it might sometimes mean doing without things one needed badly.

She sat in her cell on the little hard stool and was suddenly very happy in the darkness. It was wonderful to have nothing, nothing at all—except God. That made her richer than the richest man on earth. She remembered how on one occasion when the water jugs had not been put back in each cell after filling, they had been changed around. The pretty little water jug she used to have had been taken by someone else, and she got a big, ugly, chipped one. That made her glad, too, for it made her even poorer and brought her closer to Jesus.

Surely, surely, he would soon let her take her vows and be truly his? But that was in his hands. She would not ask even for that now, only that his will should be done, however hard it was.

15. *The Nun*

THE TIME of waiting was coming to an end at last. Canon Delatröette had given up the struggle, and September 8, 1890 was fixed as the date for Thérèse to take her vows. It was a full eight months later than it should have been. Her father was worse and was not able to come and see her, though he would not have been able to come to the ceremony anyway, because it was a private one. He would, she hoped, come two weeks later when she received the black veil.

She went into retreat for ten days beforehand. The fold of her white novice's veil was pulled forward so that her face was hidden, she was excused from work, and spent her time praying and reading. One of her favorite books was one by the great Carmelite St. John of the Cross, in which he talked of the life of prayer as if it were the climbing of a steep mountain, the Mountain of Carmel. The great saints, thought Thérèse, climbed straight up to God, fixing their eyes on the mountaintop. For her the way seemed dark; it was as if Jesus were leading her through a tunnel from which she could not see the top of the mountain. She knew only that she was getting nearer to it, for God himself was guiding her through the darkness. In a note that she wrote to Sister Marie of the Sacred Heart, she spoke of this darkness which stopped her seeing the lovely things her Bridegroom had prepared for her: "Do you think this worries me? Quite the opposite. I am happy to follow my Bridegroom simply for love of him and not for the sake of his gifts. All by himself he is so beautiful, so attractive, even when he does not speak, even when he hides himself. Do you understand your little girl? I am tired of the happiness of this earth. I want nothing but my Beloved alone."

There were practical details to arrange and a lot of people to write to who would want to know the date of her profession. She decorated the statue of the Child Jesus with flowers and candles; but when she saw the new pink candles that had been prepared, she paused and then put them away again. Instead she took out the old ones that had burned there on the day of her clothing. They had been pink and pretty then, her father had been there, and everyone had been happy. Now the candles were faded, just as earthly happiness had faded from the hearts of the five sisters. "Is there still any rose-colored happiness on earth for Father's 'little queen'?" she wrote in a note to Marie. "No, there is nothing left but the joy of Heaven . . . which is the real thing."

On the day before a profession, it is the custom for the nuns to gather in the choir, to spend the last hours of the day praying for the Sister who is to make her vows. Now it was Thérèse's turn, and they all came to the choir to pray with her and for her. For Thérèse the vigil was the end of a day filled with doubts and fears. As they knelt in the choir, it seemed to Thérèse that, after all, God did not want her to be a nun. It was all no good, she had no business in Carmel, she must go, and go at once.

It was a terrible moment. What should she do? At least she must go and tell the novice mistress; she owed her that last obedience, although she felt a violent dislike of the idea of telling her.

She got up from her place and signed to Mother Marie of the Angels that she must speak to her. Together they left the choir, and out in the cloisters it took Thérèse a few minutes to pull herself together and explain. She had no vocation, she said, she must leave at once.

Her white face was full of misery, and Mother Marie was deeply sorry for her. But she had prepared many novices for profession, and she knew the kind of last-minute panic that seizes on people committed to a difficult undertaking like this. Also she knew Thérèse and was sure that she, of all people, was led by God.

Her kind eyes crinkled at the corners as she looked at the poor girl's worried face, and to Thérèse's astonishment Mother Marie began to laugh. Then Thérèse suddenly laughed, too. Everything was all right.

They went to the Prioress, who was very kind. After that Thérèse felt perfectly at peace; she knew where God wanted her to be. When they all went to bed that night, she slept as peacefully as a baby in its own cot.

The next day, quietly happy, she took her place in the procession from the choir to the chapter. As they passed along the open cloisters, hundreds of swallows, gathering for their flight to warmer countries, swooped down in a great arc over the convent, almost brushing the gray walls with their wings as they passed. It seemed a good sign to Thérèse.

In the chapter, in the presence of the whole community, she pronounced the vows that bound her to God forever.

She made the vow of poverty. No human being has any

certainty of keeping material things or the power to claim them as his forever, but the vow accepts this and makes all possession a deliberate gift of love to God. The vow of chastity renounces marriage and family life, so that, by accepting in advance the loneliness that is the lot of everyone in some degree, that loneliness may be filled with love. The vow of obedience, also, accepts the fact that man has no power to arrange his own fate, and by submitting willingly to the Superior, the nun gives up the right even to try to have things her own way, but resolves to find love in whatever comes. By these vows the ordinary state of worried, lonely, and weak human beings ceases to be just something people have to put up with. It can become, moment by moment, an act of love.

All this Thérèse promised solemnly. But in return for this gift, she demanded such great gifts as a queen might ask from a king. She wanted all sinners to discover peace and love in conversion, all the souls of the dead to be with God. She prayed for Céline and that Léonie might find happiness as a nun of the Visitation. For herself she asked chiefly that she should never offend God by any deliberate sin. She had written down the things she wanted on a piece of paper which she carried inside her habit: "Let me die for you a martyr," she wrote. "Grant me martyrdom of soul or body, or better still, grant me both. Grant that I keep my vows perfectly, that no one may trouble about me, that I may be trampled underfoot like a tiny grain of sand."

At the end of the day she laid before Our Lady's statue the wreath of roses she had received after the ceremony. Standing at the window of her cell before she went to bed, she looked up into the darkness and thought of Heaven. She thought that perhaps it would not be so very long before she was allowed to follow her heavenly Bridegroom to his Father's house, to be with him forever.

Two weeks later, on September 24, she was given the black

veil, and this time everything went wrong. Her father had
been a little better; they had hoped he would be able to
come. But suddenly the day before the ceremony, news came
that he was worse again; he could not come to bless his
"queen." The Bishop, Monseigneur Hugonin, who was such
a friend of hers, should have come to bless the veil and give
it to her; at the last moment, she heard he could not come
either. It seemed as if the day itself was wearing a black veil,
thought Thérèse, and the worst thing was that the strength
which God had usually given her when things went badly
suddenly seemed to trickle away, leaving her weak and helpless. She cried, just as she used to do, and some of the other
nuns showed very clearly how silly they thought her. Still,
God must have a good reason for disappointing her, and she
told herself that she should learn from her own weakness and
tears over the upsetting of her plans that the strength she had
shown in the past was not something she could count on; it
was a gift that, like other gifts, might be taken away. She
must put her trust in God alone. And if her own wishes had
been disappointed, what about Céline, left behind, although
she too longed to be in Carmel? Thérèse decided to write to
her sister. Céline was having a far worse time, really—unable
to help her father herself and yet unable to follow Thérèse
into the convent in case he should need her later on. She
needed all the comfort that her sister's letter could bring
her. Céline did not even have the comfort of Léonie's company, for Léonie had gone for the second time to the convent
of the Visitation to try her vocation there.

The elder Guérin girl was getting settled, too. Jeanne got
married only a week after Thérèse's profession day, to a
young doctor called la Néèle. When she got back from their
honeymoon, Jeanne came rushing to visit her cousin Thérèse
in the convent. She scarcely stopped talking during the whole
of her time in the parlor. She could not say enough about
her husband, how good and how handsome he was, what

fun it was to look after his house, to take care of him and make him proud to have such a wife!

Thérèse listened quietly, congratulated her cousin, and wished her every happiness. After Jeanne had gone she was thoughtful. What a lot of trouble this young wife took to please her husband. But if Jeanne could do so much, she could do as well—or better. No one shall say, she said to herself, that a woman in the world does more for her husband, who is only a man, than I do for my dear Jesus.

With new energy, she was determined never to miss a chance of serving the Lord, who had so greatly honored her.

It was not very easy. The darkness of spirit seemed to have become her permanent state, and also she was depressed and worried. She began to wonder whether her small efforts and sacrifices were really any good; she was so weak and useless, so full of petty faults. As before, she thought over her faults until they seemed really dreadful. Fortunately she was very busy, for early the following year she was given the job of assistant sacristan. She had to arrange the vestments and altar linen and see that they were clean and repaired, to clean and polish the chalice and other altar vessels and the candlesticks, and to see that they were all ready for Mass each day or for Benediction. That was work she loved. She was like Our Lady, she thought, getting ready the clothes in which to wrap Child Jesus. Sometimes, when she was filling the ciborium with the small altar breads which the priest would consecrate to become the Body of Christ, she would look at her own face reflected in the shining gold bowl before she put them in, thinking that in a way she was leaving her reflection where soon the precious Body of her Lord would lie. She took endless trouble to see that the vessels shone like mirrors and that the linen was spotless and beautiful.

As for her own clothes, that was a different matter. Her habit was the oldest, thinnest, most darned of any, and besides it did not fit her. But she took it with a smile and thanks. The rope-soled canvas sandals (called in Carmel by the Spanish name of *alpargates* because the great reformer of the Order, St. Teresa of Avila, was Spanish) were picked out at random; they were old when she got them, and for poverty's sake she wore them until they nearly fell off her feet from sheer age. But she always looked so contented that no one bothered about her. It was the same with her food. She had a round face and a cheerful expression, so: "She's young and healthy," said the kitchen Sisters. "No need to worry about her." And they passed on to her heated-up bits and pieces that other people did not like. She never complained, but of course this meant that she was getting even less nourishing food than the others, although she was young and still growing. At that time much less was known about what food people need to keep healthy; no one meant any harm, but such a thing would never be allowed to happen in a convent now.

Thérèse had plenty of common sense, and if she had realized how dangerous to her health all this was, she would have mentioned it to the Prioress, and something would have been done at once. As it was, she did not realize it, nor did anyone else, and she just accepted it all and gratefully offered these little sacrifices to God.

The discomfort and bad food made her worries even worse, for nothing more easily makes people feel depressed than bad feeding. Sometimes it did not seem much good to go on struggling.

The autumn came, and in October it was the time for the community retreat. The priest who came to talk to the nuns during their retreat was called Father Alexis, and they had heard that he was very good at converting sinners and preaching to working people in the world.

Thérèse felt more depressed than ever. If she tried to explain her troubles to him, she thought, he would just think them too small and silly to bother about.

At the beginning of the retreat, the nuns went to talk to him one by one, and Thérèse went too, with a sinking heart. But as soon as she was alone with him, she knew that the man on the other side of the grille would not think her foolish, but would understand. At last she could tell someone. She told him all of it—how useless she felt, how her weakness and faults must be keeping her from God, how she seemed to live in perpetual darkness. What could she do? What use was she?

Father Alexis listened quietly to everything she told him, the long tale of tiny faults that, he saw, were stopping her from really going to God with her whole heart. He swept away all her hesitations. "Your faults do not cause God sorrow," he said firmly, and Thérèse gasped. Could it be true? She had so much hoped so, but had not dared believe it. "Speaking to you as God's representative," went on Father Alexis, "I assure you that he is very satisfied with your soul."

She left the parlor full of new courage and happiness. Her faults did not cause God sorrow, because they were simply the result of being human, of being weak, like a child. Good mothers, thought Thérèse, do not punish their children for falling down, for being clumsy, or getting dirty, because these things are just part of being a child—they cannot help it. Mothers don't worry about these things at all. They know that their children love them just the same. God is like that, she thought. Only he is much more understanding than even the best of mothers. From now on she could go forward without fear, quite sure that God loved her and wanted her love. Those small faults, instead of worrying her, would help her by reminding her how weak she was, how she could do good only with God's help.

It was not long after this retreat that old Mother Geneviève lay dying. It was she who had so much wanted Thérèse to enter and had been snubbed by Canon Delatröette. She had been ill in the infirmary for a long time, and Thérèse was very fond of her and often went to see her; the dying foundress of the convent and the youngest of the community were great friends.

On December 5 of the next year, 1891, the bell called all the nuns to the infirmary. For two hours they knelt around the old nun's bed praying, and Thérèse, who loved her so much, was worried because she could feel no sorrow; she only got sleepier and sleepier as the slow minutes passed. At last the humble and holy soul of Mother Geneviève passed into Heaven—Thérèse was sure she went straight to Heaven —and at that moment, instead of dull drowsiness, a great joy filled Thérèse. It was, she thought, a present from Mother Geneviève—a present from the glory of Heaven.

That evening she went down to the choir, where the body of the foundress was lying, surrounded by the flowers that Thérèse herself had arranged as part of her work as sacristan. On the old nun's face lay a tear, still undried, that she had noticed there as she watched by the deathbed. Gently, she wiped it away with a little piece of linen and then went back to her cell. That piece of linen would be her treasure; it would remind her that death is not sad, but glorious, for those who love God.

A few nights later she went to bed as usual after Matins and Lauds. Sometimes in those days, she dreamed about the fields and woods, the winding river and the wide sea— all the things she never saw now. But that night it was different. She dreamed that Mother Geneviève was giving to each of the nuns some little keepsake, something that had belonged to her, but when she came to Thérèse her hands were empty. There is nothing for me, thought Thérèse sadly in her dream. But the old nun looked at her lovingly. "To you, I leave my heart," she said.

Within a few weeks the quiet life of the convent was fearfully changed by an epidemic of flu which swept across Europe at that time. It was a very serious kind, and people died in great numbers. Almost everyone in the convent got it, and three died. Thérèse had only a slight attack, and she and two others struggled to nurse the more seriously ill and to keep the convent reasonably clean and tidy. Thérèse, herself still weak from the fever, washed and fed the sick and cleaned their cells, did all the usual sacristan's work and the endless extra jobs the ill nuns would otherwise have done. One morning early she woke up with a sudden knowledge that one of the sick nuns, Sister Magdalen, was dead. (It was odd how often she "knew" things like that, without any idea how the knowledge had got into her mind.) She got up and went to the nun's cell along the still dark corridor. Sister Magdalen lay peacefully on her bed, fully dressed. Thérèse quietly fetched a blessed candle from the sacristy and put a wreath of roses on the head of the dead Sister. It was all so peaceful, she thought, not the least bit frightening. These nuns went to God without fear or fuss, as if they passed into another room to meet the Friend they had known and served all their lives.

During this time, Canon Delatröette came often to visit the nuns in their difficulties, and he saw Thérèse going about her work, serene, efficient, working hard yet always patient and kind. He was astonished, and as he was an honest man in spite of his obstinacy, he admitted at last that he had been wrong about Thérèse. After that he was never tired of praising her.

At last the epidemic died down; those who had survived gradually got better, and life in the convent returned to normal. For a while longer, though, the convent chaplain allowed Thérèse to go on receiving holy communion every day, a privilege he had granted her to help her through the dark days of illness and death. That was wonderful, even though she herself felt nothing but a drowsy emptiness. It did not matter, she told herself. She did not want to receive communion for her own pleasure, but for love of Christ, so her feelings at the time were not important. It really was rather shaming to be so sleepy at the time of prayer, but she could not help it—try as she would, the drowsiness crept over her. After all, she thought, parents do not stop loving their child because it falls asleep; and God loved her still, asleep or awake, as long as she did her best.

After the flu was over, Thérèse's term of office as sacristan ran out, and for a time there was no special job for her, so she was told to help in the studio, where some of the nuns painted little pictures or illuminated cards, which were sold to help keep the community. She did as she was told and enjoyed it very much. She had always wanted to draw and paint like Pauline, and the little pictures she did were surprisingly well done. Everyone was delighted and surprised, for she clearly had talent as an artist. Unfortunately her talent had never been trained; she knew nothing about anatomy (that would have been thought a very improper thing for a well-brought-up girl to study). The pictures which were popular at that time among the pious were ones in which holy people were shown with eyes cast up to Heaven, smiling coyly or weeping large tears. Their faces and hands were so smooth that they lacked all character, their bodies so rounded and soft that one couldn't imagine them moving, because, under the pastel-colored draperies, they clearly had neither bone nor muscle to move with. These were the only pictures that Thérèse had ever looked at with any care, and she thought them lovely because everyone else did. The wonderful painting and sculpture she had seen in Italy had made no real impression on a mind full of one idea only— her visit to the Holy Father. So when she herself came to paint, it was the sugary pictures of her childhood memories that she tried to imitate. She imitated them well, much too well, and the nuns, full of admiration, got her to decorate the wall of a small oratory in the convent. On it she painted a group of baby angels scattering flowers around the Blessed

Sacrament. She used soft pretty colors and lots of soft fleecy clouds to hide the bits of the angels that she could not manage. She did it because she was told to and was not at all disturbed by the praise and excitement, though, of course, she was pleased to find how delighted everyone was with her work.

As well as painting, she wrote verses, and when the nuns found this out, they often asked her to write words which they sang on feast days to the tunes of popular songs. Some were charming, though having to stick to the rather silly tunes made the writing difficult. Her best poems were the ones she suddenly felt she had to write and scribbled down in a hurry on half a sheet of scrap paper or on the back of an envelope.

16. *In Charge of Novices*

IN FEBRUARY, 1893, Mother Marie Gonzaga's time as Prioress came to an end, and in her place Sister Agnes of Jesus was elected. Thérèse was very glad, sure that her sister's firmness and loving discipline would make her a good Prioress, as they had made her a good "mother" to her little sister. The new Prioress appointed Mother Marie Gonzaga as mistress of novices and Thérèse herself as her assistant. This was hard for Thérèse. As assistant, she naturally could not decide alone what was best for the novices, but had to work under the novice mistress and according to her ideas. But Mother Marie was an arrogant, touchy, and changeable woman who could not bear anyone else to get credit and would be likely to try to undo whatever Thérèse appeared to have achieved. And apart from this, Thérèse felt that at twenty-one she herself was too young and inexperienced for such a difficult and delicate task. Some of the novices who were to be in her charge were older than she was herself. Thérèse prayed. "You see, Lord," she said, "that I am too little to feed your children. If you want me to give each one, on your behalf, what she needs, then fill my hands, and without leaving your arms, without so much as turning my head, I will pass on your riches to those who come to me for food."

That was what she asked, and that was how it worked out, for she found that she always knew just what to say and when to say it.

That did not make the task easy. She often had to say things she hated saying, but it was her job, and she was determined to do it. She set out to teach the novices what she herself had learned—that to be holy does not mean doing great deeds for God's glory, but the daily round of dull and ordinary actions and words and thoughts, of joys and little pleasures, of small pains or disappointments, all of them offered to God. This meant constant and courageous self-denial. There was nothing easy about such a way of living, though it was so simple that anyone could understand it. But Thérèse often expressed her really hard and courageous ideas in simple, even childish words, partly because that was the way she was used to hearing people talk about spiritual things and partly in order to help the novices to feel they really could manage to do what God was asking of them. She explained to them that the way she was showing them was like an elevator that God had made for little, ordinary people who were not strong enough to climb the steep stairs to Heaven!

Her first charges were two lay Sisters who had been her companions, and they were not pleased to have her as a teacher. She was very strict, and they did not like it at first. She noticed the smallest failings, and when she had cause to find fault, she never soothed the weeping culprit afterward—that would only make her soft. Thérèse felt that if a girl were left alone, she would be forced to turn to God, see her faults, and be humble. At the same time, Thérèse allowed and even encouraged them to find fault with her in return, and they were not slow to find things in her that they did not like. Thérèse listened and acknowledged her weakness and promised to do better, and the resentful novices were ashamed, impressed by her humility, and finally began to love her, for they saw that she really did everything for their good, at whatever cost to herself.

In the warm summer weather the novices took their turn at the washing, walking to the laundry past the flower beds, and one of them dawdled, enjoying the flowers and the fine weather. "Is that how you would hurry if you had a family of children to feed and needed to work for a living?" said a voice in her ear, and the novice found herself briskly led to the washtub.

But it was Thérèse herself who took the hottest place and did the dirtiest work. When one of the others splashed her, she longed to tell her to stop it, but that would be to miss the chance of offering a sacrifice to God. It was impossible to take no notice, so she set about enjoying it instead and persuaded herself that it was rather fun to have her face splashed with dirty water.

One of the novices polished her cell with linseed oil, and Thérèse, who always chose the plainest and ugliest things for herself, made her scrub it all off again. Laziness, self-pity, any kind of self-indulgence—Thérèse pounced on such small faults like a terrier and worried at them in her talks with the novices. It worked, and the one she had scolded the day before would come and tell her so. "You were quite right to be so short with me yesterday," said one humbly. "I was very annoyed about it at first, but I thought it all over afterward, and I saw how right you were. When I left you, I thought that was the end," she admitted, "and I said to myself, 'I am going to tell our Mother that I will have nothing more to do with Sister Thérèse of the Child Jesus,' but I knew it was the devil who put this thought into my head, and I had an idea you were praying for me. Everything is clear now, and I have come back. I want you to enlighten me."

The girl was right when she thought that Thérèse was praying for her; she was always praying for the girls in her charge. Often she felt that talking was useless, that she could do nothing with a difficult case. Then she prayed, not with a lot of words and anxiety, but with a relaxed and peaceful longing and desire for the victory of goodness and love. The answer always came. Sometimes things sorted themselves out without any further help; sometimes she knew just what to say.

"You seem to have an answer for everything," said a novice during their instruction time. "I thought you were going to be caught out this time. Where do you find it all?" Thérèse smiled and told them the secret. But what about the times when she could not pray, when her soul seemed as dry as a stream bed in summer? She repeated the Lord's Prayer, very slowly, she told them, and that alone was enough.

One of them came to her cell one day during their free time and found her sewing, but the novice noticed that there were tears in her eyes. In answer to the startled questions, Thérèse looked up smiling. "It is so wonderful to be able to call God 'Our Father! Our Father!' "

The cold weather came once more, and the nuns shivered in the chilly cloister and tucked their hands inside their wide sleeves, huddling as they scurried in from the misty garden. But not Thérèse, who forced herself to walk upright and smiling when the wind whistled down the passages and cut through the cloth of her habit. Her hands were covered with chilblains, but when she sat down she did not tuck them in her sleeves but spread them out on her lap. At night she lay awake, shivering under her thin blankets until dawn. If she had told the Prioress how much she felt the cold, she would have been given more blankets at once, but she never did, for her only wish was to prove to God by suffering how much she loved him. It would have been much more sensible to have asked, but her love of God was not sensible—she could be, at times, very headstrong and foolish. But, then, the love that made the Son of God suffer a criminal's death for the sake of people who mostly never thanked him—that could be called foolish, too, and Thérèse would be foolish with Jesus. She accepted gladly all the suffering each winter brought, and she taught others to do the same.

At Christmas the nuns gave each other tiny presents, often little cards painted in the studio, where Thérèse's paintings were much admired. But one of the novices was always crying about nothing and being sorry for herself, even while they worked at their painting. Finally Thérèse seized one of the little shells they used for mixing paints and pushed it into the novice's hand. "If you must cry, then cry into that," she commanded. The poor girl began chasing teardrops from one eye to the other as she cried, and soon she and all the rest were laughing so much that tears were impossible. After that, Thérèse made her get out the shell whenever she began to cry, and she was very soon cured. Thérèse made all of them laugh, so that if she could not come to recreation, to liven things up with stories and imitations of people, the other nuns were disappointed. "There will be no laughter today," they said. "Sister Thérèse is not here."

Early in the year 1894, Pauline celebrated her first feast as Prioress, and Thérèse painted a special picture in oils in honor of the occasion. It showed the Child Jesus asleep and above his head the lance and nails and the crown of thorns, the signs of his Passion, as if even then he dreamed of it, but was not disturbed. It was not a good picture. Thérèse knew that herself and said so in a letter she wrote to go with it, explaining what it was about. But she hoped her sister would like it all the same.

Then a serious blow came. Céline heard from Father Pichon. He asked her, when her father died, to come and work with him on the missions in Canada, because he was sure the nuns would never admit four sisters to the same convent. Poor Céline had promised not to tell her sisters about this, but she did try to hint that she might have to go away, so as to prepare them. It would mean that the two sisters who had always been so close to each other would be parted for the rest of their lives, but neither of them complained. If that should be God's will, then it was good. Meanwhile their father was failing fast; it could not be long before the end came, and the three Carmelite sisters waited anxiously for news.

The warm summer days passed slowly and in the evening, during the time of the Great Silence, Thérèse sat on the terrace and watched the setting sun shine through the leaves of the chestnut trees. She thought about Céline, who would soon be free. If only she were near me, she said to herself, only perhaps it would be too much happiness. But day by day she became more certain that Céline would be joining her.

"The more I think about it, the more sure I am that you will come," she wrote to her sister on July 18. "Do not be afraid. Here more than anywhere else you will find the cross and martyrdom [more than on a mission in Canada, she thought]. We will suffer together, just as in the old days Christians banded together to give each other courage when the time of testing came. Then Jesus will come and take one of us, and the other will have to stay a little longer in banishment and sorrow. But listen . . . Jesus will never separate us. If I die before you, you needn't think that I shall go far from you—in fact, we shall be closer than ever. In any case, don't worry, I'm not ill—in fact, I've got an iron constitution; only

God can break iron as easily as pottery. But this is all childish nonsense. Let's not bother about the future."

On July 29, Monsieur Martin died, peacefully, with Céline beside him. At the end he seemed to recognize her and thank her silently, though for a long time before that he had not known her.

Although they were sad, his five daughters were also glad, for his sake. He had suffered for a long time with great patience, and they had no doubt at all that he was with God.

Céline was free at last. Should she follow her sisters or go to Canada? There were several nuns in Carmel who did not want her. Carmelite convents are never very big, and four sisters might make a group and try to run things—three, they said, were quite enough. One nun, especially, was against the idea; she said that nothing would make her change her mind. Thérèse wanted only God's will. But just as she had done when she had wanted to get into Carmel herself, she still often thought that God must want what she wanted, and now more than anything she wanted Céline beside her. She was sure that Father Pichon was wrong, that Céline must not go to Canada, and Marie agreed with her. All the three Carmelite sisters prayed urgently, while at the Guérins' country house at La Musse, where their father had died, Céline waited and wondered. But Sister So-and-so (we do not know her name) refused to be moved by entreaties.

In the morning at Mass, Thérèse knelt in her place, her face hidden by the black veil that was lowered after communion to make a little tent in which she could be alone with God. "You know, Jesus, how much I wanted our father's trials to bring him straight to you," she told Our Lord. "I long to know if this wish has been granted. I do not ask you to tell me yourself. I only want a sign. You know what that Sister feels about Céline's entering, so if she no longer objects I will take it as a sign that Father is in Heaven."

But, to her, Heaven seemed as far away as ever. She felt

nothing, but she believed. When she tried to thank God after communion, she felt nothing but sleepiness and boredom, but she was content to think that the angels and saints were continually thanking God. So, during this thanksgiving time, she stayed quietly, trying to keep her mind on God and praying for Céline. At last, at the Prioress's knock, they filed out of the choir.

In the passage, Thérèse ran into the Sister who had made all the difficulty. She called Thérèse to her in a most friendly way and took her to her own room, where she talked about Céline and made it clear that she no longer had any objection to her coming to Carmel. It was clear that she was much moved, and they talked together for several minutes. As soon as she could, Thérèse slipped back into the choir for a moment. Her prayer had been granted—her father was in Heaven, and Céline would soon be with her.

On September 14, Céline joined her sisters in Carmel, and it was Thérèse, the assistant novice mistress, who was told to take the new postulant to her cell.

That Christmas the four sisters were together again for the first time since Pauline had left the family for Carmel twelve years before. At recreation the sisters for once were standing together, and Thérèse, gayer than ever in the happy days of Christmas, began to talk of Christmas at *Les Buissonnets*, when she was a child. "Do you remember . . . ?" the Yule log, the shoes stuffed with little parcels, the cribs, midnight Mass, the old Christmas legends and songs. They listened fascinated; she made them see it all again.

"Mother Prioress," said Sister Marie of the Sacred Heart suddenly, "she should write all this down!" But Thérèse said it was nonsense, what a waste of time, as if she had nothing better to do than chatter about herself, let alone put it all on paper! Mother Agnes agreed, but Sister Marie would not be put off. In the end she got her way, and the Prioress ordered Thérèse to spend her free time writing down her memories of childhood. She had a year to do it in. It had to be ready by January 20, 1896.

She was given a child's exercise book with brown covers and rough, cheap paper, and before she began her work she knelt and asked the Mother of God to help her. Every day when the nuns were free to go to their cells after the midday recreation, Thérèse pulled her little stool out from the wall to stop herself from leaning against it, settled her sloping writing case on her lap, and began to write in the exercise book. She began at the beginning and wrote everything down just as it came into her head, without any division into paragraphs or chapters—her small, fine, upright writing covering every corner of the page.

She did all her other work as well, of course. Under her care, Céline was prepared to receive the habit of a novice. The date was February 5, 1895. She was given the name of Sister Geneviève of St. Teresa, after Thérèse's old friend Mother Geneviève, who had founded the convent. In the novitiate the older sister listened obediently to the teaching of the younger. There was only one thing they both wanted: to love God beyond everything and to give all they had to him.

17. *The Offering*

A^T TWENTY-TWO years old Thérèse was no longer the chubby, energetic girl who had fought her way into Carmel. Tall, rather thin now, her face was pale between the white folds of her toque. Above the strong, obstinate chin, firm lips, and straight little nose, her dark eyes were always ready to light up with laughter at a joke, but sometimes they were a little sad. Loving God more and more as she did, she was also more and more aware that many people did not, that their lives were empty of love and remained stunted and unhappy. All she could do was to try harder than ever to make her own life as loving as possible. Day by day, minute by minute, she gave herself to God, never missing a chance of sacrifice, never relaxing in her fight, her whole life an effort to keep nothing for herself. No one noticed. She was always smiling and pleasant, ready to joke and laugh, always obliging and helpful to everyone. They thought, because she smiled, that God made everything easy for her, that she never had to struggle, but that was one more humiliation to make her more like Christ, who was always misunderstood, never able fully to show his love. She was very alone, for she would not let herself be much with her sisters, who might have understood her.

One day in early summer she was thinking about some of the saints who had offered themselves as victims to the justice of God, asking him to punish them instead of the sinners who had deserved his anger. It was a wonderful thing to do, she thought, but somehow she did not feel that she wanted to do that herself.

Ever since there were men on earth, they have had the idea of offering sacrifice. They wanted to link their lives to the world of the sacred, the reality beyond sight that gives meaning to the world we see. Their gifts of animals or of food, the victims for their sacrifice, were offered as a sign that the men who offered them wanted to share in the life of God. When they felt they had done wrong and offended their God, they offered victims as a sign of repentance so that they would once more be linked to the life beyond. For Christians, these old sacrifices are summed up and completed in Christ, who is the real link with the sacred, the life of God. But many Christians, in trying to explain their desire to share in Christ's work of setting free God's life in men, have used the old sacrifices as a sign. They have spoken of Christ as the Victim—and of themselves as victims with him, because they shared his love, even to death. Thérèse understood this, but she did not like the idea that the Victim, Christ, offered himself simply in order to satisfy God's justice, as if God were not love itself, living in men's hearts, but a sort of heavenly Judge, waiting to reward or punish, a being remote and uncaring. Christ is the expression of God for human beings, and his offering was an offering of love, for love. Thérèse wanted to share in this offering, and to express her desire she also used the old sacrifices as a symbol.

"O God," she prayed, "must your love stay unwanted forever in your heart? It seems to me that if you found souls offering themselves to your love as sacrifices, you would burn them up quickly, happy that the rays of your boundless tenderness were no longer closed up in your heart. . . . O Jesus, let me be your happy victim, burn me up in the fire of love, your little sacrifice!"

It was as if the love of God were a great reservoir, full of water, but the people in the valley below were dying because they were too ignorant or lazy to use it. But if a channel were built from the reservoir, then the water could flow down, irrigate the valley, and save the people. That was her vocation. She, Thérèse, would let the love of God flow into her, and through her to others, to bring them to God. What did it matter if she felt nothing? The water was not for her; she only carried it.

She went to Mother Agnes's cell to ask her permission to offer herself as a victim to the merciful love of God. The Prioress looked up at the face of her little sister and saw that the love in her had even changed her face, so that it seemed to be lighted up from within. Wondering and much moved, Mother Agnes gave her permission.

Thérèse went to her cell and wrote out the words in which she wanted to make her offering, then she asked that a learned priest should approve what she had written. The Prioress showed it to the priest, and he approved it, altering only one word.

June 9 was the feast of the Blessed Trinity, and on that day Thérèse took the sheet of paper to Mass. In the Eucharist, Catholics believe that Christ's sacrifice of himself is recalled and made present under the signs of bread and wine, which are shared and eaten. So those who share this meal may also share in Christ's love. This is the love that, by complete giving, transformed the man Jesus Christ, so that he became, in his Resurrection, the "first among many brethren" who share his love and his work and so his glory. Thérèse's offering gave her a special and conscious share in this work, and so it was during the celebration of the Eucharist that she made her own offering. The prayer in which she made it was long, but she needed and meant every word. This is part of what she said: "O my God, most Holy Trinity, I want to love you and make you loved, to work for the glory of the Church by saving souls on earth and by freeing those that suffer in Purgatory. I want to accomplish your will perfectly and to reach the glory which you have prepared for me in your kingdom; in a word, I want to be a saint, but I know how helpless I am, so I beg you, O my God, to be yourself my holiness.

". . . after my exile on earth, I hope to be always with you in my homeland, but I do not want to collect merits for Heaven. I want to work only for your love, for my only aim is to please you . . . and to save souls who will love you forever. At the close of this life, I shall appear before you with empty hands, for I do not ask you, Lord, to count my works. All our good deeds are stained in your sight. So I want to be clothed with your own justice and to receive from your love yourself to be mine forever. I long for no other throne, no other crown but you, my Beloved.

"In your sight, time is nothing; one day is like a thousand years. In a moment you can make me ready to appear before you.

"So that my life may become an act of perfect love, I offer myself as a sacrificial victim to your merciful love, imploring you to burn me up ceaselessly and to let the flood-waters of your infinite tenderness flow into my soul, so that I may become a martyr of your love, O my God.

"May this martyrdom at last kill me, after having made me ready to appear before you, and may my soul throw itself at once into the unending embrace of your merciful love.

"O my Beloved, at every beat of my heart I want to make

this offering again, an endless number of times, until the shadows fade away and I can tell you of my love face to face forever!"

After Mass she folded the sheet carefully and put it in between the pages of the Gospels, a very small volume that she had chosen especially so that she could carry it with her always inside her habit. From that moment, she knew that she belonged to Jesus in a very special way. From moment to moment, she lived and moved in the depths of God's love.

When a few days later she went to the chapel to follow the Stations of the Cross, a strange thing happened which she found it impossible to describe afterward. She felt herself pierced by anguish that was at the same time glorious and sweet. "I felt myself wounded with a dart of fire so burning that I thought I should die," she told Mother Agnes wonderingly. "I do not know how to explain—nothing I could compare it to would show you how intense that flame was. It seemed as if an invisible power plunged me entirely into fire. But what a fire . . . how sweet it was," she added softly. "If it had lasted a minute, even a second more, my soul would have parted from my body. . . ."

But she was still on earth, and her soul was now as dark as it had been before. Mother Agnes listened quietly and said nothing. She remembered saints whose lives she had read—things like that happened to them. But this girl who stood before her, trying to explain what could not be explained, was her sister, the child she had brought up. So Mother Agnes watched and listened and said nothing, but Thérèse knew that God had accepted her sacrifice.

No one else noticed any difference. But, then, Thérèse's sacrifices were always quiet and private, for no one will notice what a person does *not* do. Not to rub her chilblained hands or bury them in her big sleeves when the frost made them itch and ache, not to shiver or crouch against the biting wind that swept down the cloister, not to dry out cold wet

stockings, not to wipe her soap-splashed face at the washtubs,
not to seek the shadiest corner in the heat of the summer,
not to complain when she got burnt or dried-up leftovers
for a meal, not to replace worn-out clothes and *alpargates,*
not to frown at a noisy Sister or avoid an irritating one, not
even to murmur or move when a Sister fastening her scapular pin drove it into her shoulder, in case the helper's feelings should be hurt—these were Thérèse's sacrifices, her way
of keeping on offering herself to God.

Two good things happened that autumn. First Marie Guérin, pretty, amusing Marie, came to join her cousins in
Carmel. It was such fun to have her cheerful face in the
Novitiate—everyone felt younger and gayer—and her lovely
voice charmed the nuns at recreation as well as in choir. But
Thérèse did not forget to write to Jeanne, who had lost her
only sister, and to her uncle and aunt. "Didn't God promise
that he who leaves father or mother or sister for his sake
shall receive a hundredfold in this life?" she wrote to Jeanne.
"Well, you did not hesitate to give up a dear sister. . . . Oh,
I know that people usually mean souls with religious vocations when they say these words, but I am sure in my heart
that they were spoken for the generous relations who sacrifice children whom they love more than themselves." She
thanked Jeanne for a present sent for her feast day. "I must
go and do the washing," she ended her letter, "and while I
rub I shall listen to our dear little imp, who will probably
sing to us." For her feast day that year happened to be a
washing day. As the nuns scrubbed and lifted the linen and
stirred and rinsed the boiler full of washing, they were
cheered by the songs of Sister Marie of the Eucharist—that
was Marie's new name.

Thérèse was rubbing away with energy when a hand on
her shoulder made her look up from her work. The Prioress
had sent for her, and she went at once to her room, wondering what this unexpected summons was about.

"I have a letter from a young man studying for the priest-hood and the African missions with the White Fathers," the Prioress explained. "He asks us to give him a spiritual sister. Listen."

The letter said that reading about the great St. Teresa, he had been inspired to ask the Carmel for a sister who would devote herself especially to his salvation and to the salvation of the souls he would be given to look after. He promised that he would always remember his new sister when he celebrated the Eucharist after he was made a priest. The Prioress had decided that Thérèse should be that sister.

Suddenly Thérèse felt as if she were walking on air. This was something she had always longed for—to have a brother a priest! Her own little brothers had died before she was born, and she had thought it was impossible, but now God was answering her prayer. He was giving her not only a priest, but one who was going to work on the missions just as she had so often longed to do herself. It was the happiest day she could remember since she was a little girl, and she began to work and pray harder than ever for the sake of her new brother.

So she had her three sisters with her, and the new novice Marie; she had her missionary brother to think of and work for. (As yet she had heard nothing from him. She knew only that he had gone to begin his period of military service, for in France students for the priesthood had to serve as well as everyone else.)

All these were in her thoughts to make that Christmas one of the happiest she had ever had. On Christmas Day the Sisters had a little party to celebrate, and Thérèse decided to write a kind of play for it, in which there was only one actor—herself. It was called *The Little Beggar of Christmas* and was to be a surprise for the nuns.

When the time came, they were all together in the recreation room. Then came Thérèse in the part of an angel, carrying the figure of Infant Jesus from the crib. First she sang a little song about the coming of the Son of God, born on earth as a baby. Then she tenderly laid the rosy little doll in the manger, and turning toward the Prioress, she knelt and offered her a basket full of folded pieces of paper. One by one the nuns came up and took one; one by one they handed them back to the angel. She opened them in turn, singing from each what the newborn King was asking from his servants. Such odd things some of them seemed for a baby to want: a star, a bunch of grapes, a mirror; but others were certainly just right: milk, a pillow, a toy, a cradle. All these things had a meaning which was explained in the little song. "Jesus would like roses," sang Thérèse:

> *I love the flower of innocence,*
> *The lily pure and white,*
> *But still the rose of penitence*
> *Blood-red is my delight.*

And certainly a baby might like sweets, but:

> *The toffees that I sing,*
> *Fit for your Heavenly King,*
> *Are made from sacrifice,*
> *From every self-denial*
> *In poverty and trial.*
> *For Jesus, these are nice!*

As for the little cradle, that was a lovely thing to offer to the Baby King:

> *This Baby's delight*
> *Is to sleep the long night*
> *From fear safely kept.*
> *If you'd cradle this Child,*
> *Our Lamb soft and mild,*
> *He'd smile as he slept.*

She sang for each Sister in turn, and they were all charmed. It was certainly a wonderful feast day, a shining light in the middle of the long, dark winter.

It seemed colder than ever this year; the icy wind made Thérèse catch her breath, and she had a permanent sore throat. (Some of the nuns teased her and said she got it from talking such a lot to the novices.) She said nothing and was sure it would get better when the warm weather came. Meanwhile she finished the story of her life for Mother Agnes, writing the last chapter in snatches, her fingers so cold and so cracked and sore with chilblains that it was hard to hold the pen. On the feast of St. Agnes, January 21, 1896, she handed her manuscript to Mother Agnes as the nuns filed into their stalls for Vespers. The Prioress took it, but she was very busy at that time, for her term of office was nearly over, and there was a lot of business to wind up. She put the manuscript in a drawer, meaning to read it later, and forgot all about it for several months. Thérèse said nothing. She would have gone on saying nothing if Mother Agnes had thrown it in the fire. What did a bit of writing matter? She had written it under obedience, and it belonged, as she herself did, to Almighty God, to be treated just as he chose.

A month later Céline—Sister Geneviève—made her profession. The evening before, Céline found an envelope in her cell addressed to "My Beloved Bride, Geneviève of St. Teresa, living in love on the Mountain of Carmel." It was postmarked "The Kingdom of Heaven," with the date "Eternity." In fact, it was another of Thérèse's odd little pious jokes. Herself almost always in darkness, so that Heaven seemed far away and unreal, she liked to make up games like this to please other people and to cheer herself up. Inside this envelope was a long letter pretending to come from Christ, written on vellum and with two coats of arms painted at the top. It was a marriage contract and began with these words: "I, Jesus, the Eternal Word, the only Son of God and of Mary the Virgin, take as my bride Céline, a princess in exile, poor and without title. I give myself to her under the name of Knight of Love, of Suffering, and of Humiliation."

It was a long letter, telling the new nun that although her present life was one of poverty and humiliation, her day of glory would come, when her Knight would reveal himself to her, and they would share forever the same throne and the same crown.

Tucked away in the bottom margin, in very small letters, was a very small joke: "Thérèse of the Child Jesus, Publisher to the Divine Knight." Thérèse meant that the brave words and promises she had written for Céline were really from God. She herself just did the writing. She played such games of a kind of grown-up "let's pretend" quite often, which was one reason why her life of endless sacrifices, of becoming always less and less, was hidden from her Sisters. They saw only her gay smile and pictures, heard her amusing stories and happy little poems at recreation, and noticed her cheerful way of helping the novices.

It was her sister, Pauline—Mother Agnes—who had given her the charge of the novices, but now her time as Prioress was almost over, and a new Prioress had to be chosen. Thérèse herself had no vote in the chapter when the nuns gathered to choose their new Mother, because not more than two nuns from the same family were allowed to vote in one Carmelite convent, and Marie and Pauline were both older than she.

After the nuns in the chapter had prayed for guidance, each one wrote down the name of the Sister she thought best fitted to rule the convent in the coming three years. They had to vote seven times before any name got enough votes, but finally it was Mother Marie Gonzaga who once more took her place as Prioress. Mother Marie decided to keep Thérèse to train the novices, for she loved her and had learned in the past three years to respect her as well. At the same time, she kept the title of novice mistress herself as before. As usual, Mother Marie could not bear to take the risk that someone else would appear to be doing better than she herself. By this new arrangement, if Thérèse did well at her job, Mother Marie could claim the credit. But Thérèse did not mind. She was careful, all through her life in Carmel, never to say or write a word of direct criticism of any of the nuns, but she was much too intelligent not to see what was wrong. If she accepted such a very unjust arrangement without complaint, it was not out of laziness or stupidity, but because she felt that more good could be done by saying nothing. When it was her job to point out faults, as with the novices, she did so. But whether she spoke out or not, she understood the reasons why people behave in stupid, mean, and unkind ways. Mother Marie Gonzaga was a strange, unhappy woman who was afraid and needed a lot of reassurance. Her need always to show her own importance made this clear. Thérèse saw through the fear and jealousy and saw underneath it a warm heart. She loved Mother Marie, and her love was returned. What mattered to Thérèse was the giving and receiving of love, not what people thought of her, and she was not in the least interested in who got the credit for her work with the novices. It is possible that she did not even notice the slight. She seemed to herself so unimportant that she was no longer disturbed by such a little thing.

When the news that Thérèse was to remain as assistant novice mistress was given to the nuns, one person in particular was very glad—one of the novices, Marie of the Trinity. She was having a difficult time during her novitiate and felt that she needed Thérèse's wise and firm guidance. Thérèse herself was delighted, because as well as giving her the charge of the novices, the Prioress made her sacristan once more, and she loved that work.

The Lent of 1896 was nearly over, and although warmer

weather was coming, Thérèse felt cold all the time. The strict fast had used up her strength, and she was very tired. Holy Week came. The convent was in mourning as the nuns followed the story of the Passion of Christ step by step. On the night of Holy Thursday, they all went to the choir to watch before the Altar of Repose. In Catholic churches on this day, there is a solemn Eucharist celebration to commemorate its institution at Christ's last supper with his disciples. Afterward the altar where it is celebrated is stripped and left bare as a sign of mourning. But some of the holy Bread —the sacramental sign of Christ's Body—is kept in order to give holy communion to the people at the Good Friday service next day. It is carried in procession and kept overnight in a side chapel or small side altar, and many people like to come and pray near it during the night. The altar is surrounded with lights and flowers as a sign that even at this sad time we are looking forward to Easter, when "death is swallowed up in victory."

In Carmel many of the nuns would watch there all night, and Thérèse would have liked also to spend the dark hours thinking of the Lord before his Passion, but Mother Marie's sharp eyes had noticed her strained face and the dark circles under her eyes. She ordered her to bed at midnight, and Thérèse bowed obediently and went. In her cell, she took off her habit, blew out the lamp, and climbed wearily onto the rustling straw mattress. She pulled the blankets up and lay quietly, staring up into the darkness. Suddenly a stream of warm liquid rushed up into her mouth, and she reached for her handkerchief to catch the flow. What had happened? Was she going to die? At the thought a great wave of excitement swept over her. She longed to find out the truth, but the lamp was out. She was supposed to be resting, so she pushed the handkerchief back under the pillow and lay peacefully until she fell asleep.

At five o'clock the rattle sounded as the Sister swung the

clapper along the passage, and as usual Thérèse got up at once. Her first thought when she woke was that good news was coming to her. Dawn was breaking as she went to the window, and by the early light she saw that her handkerchief was soaked with blood. She knew little about medicine, but she knew what that meant: she was ill, with an illness that was usually fatal. On this Good Friday it seemed to her that Christ was calling her to share his death—but the call was still faint and far off.

Meanwhile it was her duty to tell the Prioress of any serious ill health. She did not count a cough and a sore throat, growing tiredness or indigestion worth reporting, but now she went to Mother Marie after Prime and the Chapter of Faults were over and, kneeling before her—as the custom was for any nun talking to the Prioress—told her plainly and quickly what had happened. "I don't feel the least tiredness or pain, Mother," she added. "Will you allow me to finish Lent as I began it?"

Mother Marie looked down at her spiritual daughter over the top of her spectacles and thought for a moment. The night before, she had sent Thérèse to bed because she looked tired. The sensible thing now would be to send her back to bed and get the doctor. But Mother Marie had got to know Thérèse well during the time the girl had been her assistant as novice mistress. She knew by now what heroism was hidden by that smile, and perhaps she had a feeling that in this case ordinary common sense was not enough. God might have other plans for this most uncommon young woman. Whatever her reasons, Mother Marie did something which seemed cruel, blind, stupid—she told Thérèse to carry on as before. Mother Agnes would have cosseted her, warmed her, dosed her; but instead of a loving sister, it was this fierce and capricious but perhaps inspired old woman who was Thérèse's Superior during her last years, and Thérèse was glad of this.

All through that day of mourning, Thérèse worked as usual. They had no food until midday and then only a very little. In the afternoon she was told to clean some windows, and while she was doing it one of the novices passed. She saw the face of her mistress gray with exhaustion, dark shadows under her eyes. The novice, horrified, burst into tears. "Please, Sister," she begged, "please let me ask our Mother to give you a rest."

Thérèse turned on her. "I forbid you even to mention it," she said almost fiercely. "Surely I should be able to bear a little tiredness on the day when Jesus suffered so much for me."

But that night when she went to bed there came again the hot stream against her lips, and again she soaked up the blood with a handkerchief and went to sleep.

18. *Letters*

ON THAT Good Friday of 1896, it seemed to Thérèse that she had seen the glory of Heaven as if through a half-open door. She wrote later: "At this time I had such a clear and living faith that the thought of Heaven was my greatest happiness." But at Easter time, when Christians celebrate the glory of Christ, who made suffering and death the way to the love of God which is Heaven, Thérèse lost that happiness, as if the half-open door had been shut in her face. However deep the darkness had been before, she had had a rocklike faith to support her, a sure hope of eternal glory and happiness at the end of the tunnel. Now she was tempted to doubt. Was God really there? Was there really a glorious future for her tormented soul? Suppose after all the struggles there was—nothing. In horror, Thérèse turned to the God who did not seem to be there.

"I believe!" she cried to him. "I do believe!" Over and over again she declared her faith. It seemed to her that she

was like the people who have no faith—very well, perhaps
her suffering would help them. She turned to God and said
with the writer of the Psalms, "Thou hast given me, O Lord,
a delight in thy doings."

These doubts did not end. Only now and then the darkness lifted for a moment, as if the tunnel in which she
walked was pierced by narrow clefts in the rocks above and
light filtered feebly through into the blackness inside. Life
in Carmel went on as usual; no one but the Prioress guessed
that there was anything much wrong with Thérèse, for she
was as quietly cheerful as ever. Not long after Easter, one of
Thérèse's novices, Marie of the Trinity, was professed. It
was a day of great happiness, for she had not been an easy
girl to train, and Sister Marie herself knew very well that
if it had not been for Thérèse, she could never have managed to persevere. Thérèse knew it, too, and though she also
knew that it was God and not she who had done the work,
she was full of joy at what had been achieved. "I feel like
Joan of Arc at the crowning of Charles VII," she said de-
lightedly to the young nun, thinking of how her favorite
heroine had stood, banner in hand, to see the crown placed
on the head of the king in whose cause she had battled so
bravely.

Then came another break in the darkness. On the night
of May 10 she fell asleep exhausted by work and the unending struggle with her doubts. Toward dawn, between
sleeping and waking, she dreamed that she was walking in
a gallery with the Prioress, when she saw three other Carmelites coming toward them wearing their white choir
cloaks and long black veils. She knew without surprise that
they came from Heaven. If only I could see the face of one
of these Carmelites, she thought in her dream, I would
be so happy. As if she had heard her, the tallest of the
three nuns came forward, and as Thérèse fell on her knees,
she covered them both with the folds of her veil so that

the kneeling girl found herself looking up into a face of unearthly beauty that seemed to shine with a soft light even under the heavy black veil. As people do in dreams, Thérèse knew at once that this was the foundress of the first reformed Carmelite convents in France, a friend of the great St. Teresa, called Anne of Jesus. The lovely face bent toward her, and the great Carmelite kissed her daughter. Gathering courage from the gentle eyes that looked into hers, Thérèse spoke to her. "Tell me, Mother, I beg you, is God going to leave me here much longer? Will he come and fetch me soon?"

The nun smiled tenderly. "Soon," she said softly. "Yes . . . soon. . . . I promise you."

"Tell me another thing, Mother dear. Does God want no more from me than the little things I do for him, and my longings? Is he pleased with me?"

As Thérèse gazed upward, the beautiful face seemed to shine with a new splendor, the grave eyes were full of love. "God asks no more from you," said the voice again, "and he is pleased with you . . . very, very pleased."

Then Thérèse felt cool hands holding her head, and loving kisses covered her face. Her heart was filled with happiness, with a joy she longed to share, so that she wanted to ask something for her Sisters. But suddenly she awoke to see the light of the spring morning slanting between the shutters onto the whitewashed wall of her cell. The dream had gone, but the memory remained. She was sure now that Heaven existed, for one of the Blessed had loved her and visited her. For a while, at least, there was peace in the heart of Thérèse.

She developed an irritating little dry cough. The mild weather seemed to do it no good, and the Prioress sent her to see the doctor on one of his visits. Dr. de Cornières examined her. Sister Thérèse of the Child Jesus looked cheerful, her cheeks were pink—not much wrong with her, thought the doctor. A cough? Yes, yes. A little tonic would put things right. Thérèse smiled and thanked him.

The tonic and extra strengthening food certainly helped. She seemed stronger, and everyone was reassured.

June brought an unexpected joy. A young man who was about to be ordained priest and sent on the foreign missions wrote to the Prioress to ask for one of her daughters as his particular helper in his work. Mother Marie Gonzaga picked Thérèse without hesitation, which shows what that shrewd old lady thought of her assistant of twenty-three. "She is the best of my good ones!" wrote Mother Marie to the young man, whose name was Roulland.

So Thérèse was given a second "brother." He was to be ordained on June 29, so she made a set of altar linen for his first Mass and gave it to Mother Marie for her feast day so that the Prioress herself should have the pleasure of sending it to the young priest. This generous action shows not only that Thérèse was quite without self-love but that she recognized the Prioress's weakness and was capable of sympathizing with it. She knew that it was fear that made Mother Marie unjust and aggressive and that when she was sure of being loved she could be generous, too, and understanding. Thérèse also wrote a polite and slightly formal letter to the Father Roulland, telling him that she would do her very best for him. "I shall be really happy to work with you to save souls," she wrote. "That is why I became a Carmelite. Since I could not be an active missionary, I wanted to be one through love and penance." She asked him to remember her in his first Mass. "For a long time I have wanted to know an Apostle who would pronounce my name at the holy altar on the day of his first Mass. I wanted to prepare the sacred linen myself, and the white Host which was destined to hide the King of Heaven. . . ." At the end of the letter, she asked him to keep secret their fellowship as apostles.

A few days later the new priest came to Lisieux and said Mass in the chapel of the Carmel. Thérèse, radiant, was sent to the parlor to speak to him afterward. The two missionaries could not see each other, for the black curtain of the grille was between them. The visit was short, and they said little. There was no need, for they understood each other well, without words. He was to leave for China in a month; she would probably never speak to him again.

Thérèse wrote a lot of letters. She wrote to poor Léonie, who was once more out of the convent where she had tried to be a nun. She was sad and lonely and no longer young. She felt that she did not do enough for God, that she was, as usual, the useless one. Thérèse wanted to encourage her. Rather late in answering her letter, she said, "There are five of us, and you know I am the smallest—so I risk seeing the letters a long time after the others, or even not at all." (She was the youngest, though she had been there longer than Céline—and Marie Guérin—and of course she never said to any of them, "I have not seen the letter." It was better to keep quiet. Even her sisters sometimes forgot Thérèse, so small had she become, "trodden underfoot like a grain of sand" as she had wished.)

"God is much kinder than you think," she wrote to Léonie. "As far as I am concerned, I find it very easy to practice perfection, because I have understood that we have only got to *catch the heart of Jesus*. Watch a child who has made his mother angry by getting in a temper or being disobedient. If he hides in a corner with a sulky expression and cries for fear of being punished, his mother will certainly not forgive his fault. But if he comes and stretches his little arms to her and smiles, saying, 'Kiss me, and I will not do it again,' don't you think his mother will lovingly hug him to her heart at once and forget what he has done? She knows quite well that her darling *will* do it again next time, but that does not matter. If he catches her heart, he will never be punished."

Thérèse was trying to express, in a way that could easily be understood, her deep conviction that faults are not important where there is love. It is true that faults separate people, prevent understanding and love, but if a person really wants to love, then in the end love is stronger than the faults. It will either overcome them or make them seem invisible, because real love is God, working in human life.

"You asked for news of my health," she ended her letter. "Well, my dearest sister, I am not coughing any more. Are you satisfied? But that will not stop God taking me when he wants to. Since I do my best to be like a small child, I have no preparations to make. Jesus will have to pay all the expenses of the journey himself, and the entrance money to Heaven! Good-bye my dear little sister! I think I love you more and more."

At the end of July, Father Roulland left for China, and before he left he wrote to Mother Marie and sent her a photograph of himself. The photographer had put him on a bit of rock, and there he sat in his long black cassock, holding a crucifix and with his black hat on his knee. His young, round face with its short beard looked stubborn, and he had frank, fearless eyes. Carmelites are not usually allowed photographs, even of close relations, but Mother Marie could sweep away little customs when she felt like it. So the Prioress suddenly turned up in Thérèse's cell. "Keep this for me in your writing case," she said, holding out the photograph. "I will take it when I need it."

Thérèse knelt and took the little picture of her "brother." "Thank you, Mother," she said, and looked up at the Prioress with a smile, for they understood each other very well. When the Prioress had gone, Thérèse sat and looked for some moments at the face of the brother God had sent her, then she put it away in her case and wrote a little note to go with it, for she knew how unusual it was for a nun to be allowed a photograph. "This photograph does not belong to me," she wrote. "Our Mother has told me to keep it in our writing case; she will take it when she needs it." But

Mother Marie never needed it, and it stayed in Thérèse's case until she herself needed it no longer.

Meanwhile she wrote to Father Roulland to speed him on his long journey. "My Brother," the letter began this time, instead of "Reverend Father," for she knew now that he would not be offended. She told him about the photograph: ". . . so while I shall cross the sea with you, you will stay near me in our poor cell! Everything around me reminds me of you. I have put a map of Su-Tshuen [the province of China where he was going] on the wall of the room where I work, and the little picture you gave me always stays near my heart in the book of the Gospels, which never leaves me." The picture was a souvenir of his ordination that he had sent. Now he was leaving his family and his home, as she had done. But Jesus had promised to those who left all "a hundredfold in this world, and in the world to come, life everlasting." She asked him also to tell her the most important dates in his life; she was always interested in dates. "Distance will never separate our souls," she went on, "even death will only make our union closer. If I go to Heaven soon, I shall ask Jesus to let me visit you at Su-Tshuen, and we will carry on our apostolic work together. In the meantime, I shall always be united to you by prayer, and I am asking Our Lord never to let me be happy when you are suffering. I would even like my Brother to have all the joys and myself all the trials—or is that selfish? Not really, since my only weapon is love and suffering, and your blade is that of preaching and of apostolic work."

The Prioress saw the letter before it was sent and added a little note of her own. "Dear Child, 'Man proposes, and God disposes,' " wrote Mother Marie. "I wanted to write you a long letter, but Jesus has given me a slight illness which prevents me from writing. Now I am nothing but an old crock, and my chest plays me tricks every now and again, but I will offer it up to win souls to whom our dear apostle will bring the Gospel. You have a very fervent helper, who will leave nothing undone to save souls. The dear child belongs entirely to God."

When Thérèse wrote to this brother, she could at last write as a grown-up person to an equal. Her letters to him are plain, dignified, occasionally amusing, always full of the heroic love that filled her life. To him she wrote without frills, without the pretty little metaphors of lambs, flowers, and toys that she used to her sisters. They all thought of her as a baby still; even to Céline she was still a "little sister," and Mother Agnes found it impossible to believe that the little girl she had trained could really be grown up. It reassured them to think like that, for how could God allow anything unpleasant to happen to their baby sister? As Marie had said to Thérèse when she was still small, "I am sure God will never make you walk by the way of suffering." It was a comforting belief, and because she knew it pleased them, Thérèse went on writing and speaking to her sisters as she had as a small child, even using baby talk when she felt they needed to be amused or comforted.

Since Mother Agnes was no longer Prioress, she had rather more time to herself that summer. One day when she was tidying some drawers, she came across the story that she had asked Thérèse to write for her. It was still lying unread in its corner, and she took it out and read it. It was charming, she thought, written in such a simple, childlike way. What a very sweet and holy girl her sister was! She showed it to Sister Marie of the Sacred Heart.

Marie had always been less sentimental than Pauline. She took little notice of the sweetly childish way in which the story was written; she saw underneath it a plain account of a life of complete self-sacrifice and love. Marie suddenly felt that she must know more. It seemed to her that, wonderful as it was, this story showed only the surface; and if that was so beautiful, what might not be hidden beneath it?

She wasted no time but took the manuscript to the Prioress. She begged her to tell Thérèse to write down what she felt now about her life as a Carmelite and about her way of living as a child before God. The Prioress agreed.

So Thérèse got out her writing case again. Without pausing, for there was no need to think out what was always in her mind, she wrote for her sister Marie about the love that filled her life, about the way she had found that led straight to the heart of love. "It is the way of childlike self-surrender, the way of a child who sleeps, afraid of nothing, in its father's arms. 'Whoever is a little one, let him come unto me,' says the Holy Spirit through the lips of Solomon, and the same Spirit of Love tells us also that 'to him that is little, mercy is granted.' . . . My darling Godmother, one can only remain silent, one can only weep for gratitude and love, after words like that. If only every weak and imperfect soul felt what this smallest of all souls, the soul of your little Thérèse, feels, no one would despair of reaching the topmost peak of the mountain of love, for Jesus does not ask for glorious deeds, but only for self-surrender and for gratitude."

As she wrote, Thérèse suddenly stopped writing as if to her sister, and turning to Jesus, she wrote for him, for only in that way could she say all that she felt. She thanked him for all the graces he had given her—"to be your bride, my Jesus; to be a Carmelite; to be, through union with you, a mother of souls." But that was not enough for her. Her love went beyond the possible. As well as her vocation to be "Carmelite, wife, and mother," as she said, she wanted also to be a soldier, a priest, an apostle, a doctor of the Church, a martyr . . . "martyrdom—that was the dream of my childhood, a dream I have kept with me in the cloister of Carmel." And she wanted not just one but every kind of martyrdom. "What can you say in face of all this foolishness, for is there a littler or weaker soul on earth than mine?" But she realized at last that all the vocations, all the great works of the saints were summed up in one word—love.

"I know I am no more than a helpless child, yet, my Jesus, it is my very helplessness which makes me dare to offer myself as a victim to your love. . . . But is there really pure love in my heart? Are my vast desires only a dream and nothing but foolishness? . . . And yet if it should happen that I never attain the heights to which my soul reaches out, I swear I shall have tasted far more sweetness in my foolishness and my martyrdom than I shall taste in the midst of eternal joys, unless you work a miracle and take from me the memory of my earthly hopes. O Jesus, Jesus, if the desire of love brings such delight, what must it be really to possess it and enjoy it for all eternity?" She was, she said, nothing but a helpless fledgling compared with the great eagles, the saints. But Jesus himself, the Divine Eagle, had come down to earth to suffer and die. "O Jesus, let me tell you with overflowing gratitude that your love goes to the lengths of madness. In the face of such madness, what can you expect save that my heart should fly out to you? How can my confidence know any limits? . . . If only, my Jesus, I could tell all *little souls* about the way beyond describing in which you came down to our level! . . . But why this desire to tell others the secrets of your love? Was it not you alone who taught them to me, and can't you make them clear to others also? I know you can, and I beg you to do so. I implore you, look upon a great number of little souls; choose in this world, I beg of you, an army of little victims worthy of your love."

Sister Marie read what Thérèse had written for her, and she was astounded. Thrilled at the greatness of the love she found there, yet afraid that such a soul could not stay long on earth, she also felt how very far she herself was from a like heroism. She wrote to Thérèse a pathetic little note. "I am afraid of the things you long for," she wrote, "which proves that I don't love Jesus as you do." And she asked her sister to write her a note to tell her if she could really hope to love like that. Thérèse wrote back at once. Her sister had misunderstood her. How could she think that her wild longings were what mattered? They were just a sort of luxury; they might even be a danger. No, it was being little that mattered, nothing else. The smaller and weaker one was, seeming even to be without virtues, even without desires for God, the easier it was for love to take control.

There was another letter to write, this time to her first spiritual brother, the young student Maurice Bellière. He had just finished his military service and had found it difficult to hold on to his wish to be a priest, in the company of all sorts of young men who not only thought such an idea silly but tried to get him to share the sort of life they thought of as "gay." What was more, to be a missionary would mean leaving the people he loved, and he was finding it all very hard. Mother Marie Gonzaga had had his letter in July, when he wrote to tell her of his troubles, but her illness prevented her from answering it, and when he wrote again to say that things were better, she told Thérèse to write for her.

To this very young brother (he was only eighteen) Thérèse did not write in the sisterly way she wrote to Father Roulland, but more as if she were the young man's mother. Her letters are tender and helpful, soothing his worries with a quiet, loving firmness. "Now that the storm is past," she told him, "I thank God for making you go through it. You see, when Jesus calls a soul to guide and to save a multitude of other souls, it is very necessary that he should give that soul some experience of the temptations and trials of life."

There seemed to be such a lot of letters to write—she couldn't *not* write them. People needed her words, her comfort, and however tired she felt, she had to get out her writing case during the short free time she had, pull her little stool away from the whitewashed wall (tiredness was no excuse for lolling), and write and write. Another long letter went off to Father Roulland in China. He had sent his list of important dates, and she was strangely moved to find that on September 8, 1890, as he prayed to the Mother of Jesus, he had suddenly felt that his vocation to the priesthood was safe after a time of terrible doubt. On that same day, she told him, a little Carmelite novice had become the bride of Christ. It had been her profession day. She remembered how she had asked her Lord to give her, as a sort of wedding present, the soul of an apostle, who would share her longings and hopes. She was delighted to hear that he was wearing Chinese dress and a pigtail—if she thought it funny, she did not say so. "I thought of Our Lord putting on human form," she wrote, a comparison not very complimentary to the Chinese people. The letter would reach him for New Year, so she sent him her New Year wishes—for his martyrdom! People might think that an odd sort of wish, she admitted, "but our only wish is to be like our beloved Master," and she asked him to pray for her other young brother.

It was almost easy to write to him, she had so much to say, if only she had not been so terribly tired. If only she could get a bit better, she might be able to go to the missions herself. The Carmelites at Hanoi in Indochina were asking for a nun from Lisieux, and someone had suggested Thérèse. To leave her home town, the convent she loved, her sisters, to live and die among strangers—that would really be a sacrifice worth offering. She had always longed to go to the mission field, and one of her favorite saints was a young missionary who had been martyred, called Théophane Vénard. He had always been cheerful, too. Perhaps, she thought hopefully, he would help her. She asked him to beg from God that she also might make his long journey and perhaps even die as he had died.

By the end of the week, it seemed to her that she had indeed had an answer to her prayer, and the answer was "no." Suddenly all the good that the extra food, the summer warmth, and Dr. de Cornières' tonic had seemed to do was over, and she was much worse. God did not want Thérèse to die gloriously on the mission field. He intended her to die slowly and unromantically in her own convent.

19. *The Last Winter*

THE PASSAGES of the convent seemed terribly long. The stairs to the dormitory seemed to grow steeper and steeper. It was difficult to get through the sacristy work, the vestments were so heavy now. It was hard, too, to be bright and amusing at recreation and to listen cheerfully to the novices' chatter. But she mustn't be gloomy, especially at Christmastime, only a few days away.

The novices were very excited over a boxful of oddments left over from a bazaar which had been held in the town to help the foreign missions. It was a deep box, and they had a wonderful time digging out pretty bits and pieces to decorate the Christmas tree. Sister Marie of the Trinity was busy fishing out toys and artificial flowers, books and pious pictures with the others. She was still in the Novitiate, for all the young nuns remained under the care of the novice mistress for a while after their profession, in order to get extra help and guidance. Thérèse watched her a little anxiously. She had been a difficult girl all along, moody, excitable, sulky, and terribly childish. The only way she seemed to make any progress was pretending to play games with Jesus. Thérèse smiled to herself as she thought of the latest one: playing at ninepins, pretending that the souls she wanted to save (and she really did want to save souls, for all her silliness) were colored ninepins that she could knock down with the ball of her love for God! But it seemed to help her to love God, and that was all that mattered.

The novices got to the bottom of the box, but one object was still there, a little wooden whipping top. Some did not like being reminded how near to their schooldays they still were, so they pretended not to know what it was. "Isn't it ugly! Whatever is it for?" they chorused.

But little Sister Marie was delighted. "But it's great fun! It'll go for a whole day without stopping, as long as it gets whipped!" And she snatched up a piece of string and quickly set the little top whirring on the floor while the others laughed. Thérèse watched quietly.

Christmas came, and after midnight Mass the nuns sang a carol before they went to their cells for their short sleep. When Sister Marie of the Trinity opened her door, she saw on her pillow the little wooden top and a note lying by it. It was addressed to "My dear little bride, who plays at ninepins on Mount Carmel." The Child Jesus was very pleased with the game, he said, but now he wanted a change; *he* wanted to play with a top. "You must be the top. I am giving you one as a model—you see it's not pretty. . . . I love you, although you are not very nice-looking, and I want you to spin all the time to amuse me. But to make a top go, it needs to be whipped. Well, then, let your Sisters do that for you, and be grateful to the ones who are bent on keeping you from slowing down. When I have played with you enough, I will carry you off where we can play without suffering." That was Thérèse playing "pretend" again, talking baby talk for the sake of a girl who still behaved rather like a baby. But the lesson was a hard one all the same, and one that Thérèse herself had learned thoroughly. She wanted to keep on "spinning" as long as she was needed, and if she could have been slowed down by unkindness and injustice, she would have slowed to a stop long before. Thérèse herself was so careful never to mention what she suffered from other people in the convent that it is difficult to realize how much she did suffer. But, later on, some of it came to light. In any family or community there may be small jealousies and outbreaks of malice. In the Carmel of Lisieux there had been, unfortunately, little of the firm and loving guidance from a wise Prioress that might have helped the nuns to overcome their uncharitableness. Although Mother Marie Gonzaga had not been Prioress for very long, she had a great deal of influence, backed up by rich relations. She encouraged a few of the nuns to form a sort of "party" of her supporters and made favorites of them. Where there should have been peace and harmony, there was rivalry and bickering, and the Martin sisters, who were among those who tried really hard to live according to the true Carmelite spirit, were not popular. But Thérèse had also managed to win Mother Marie Gonzaga's affection, and that did not endear her to the nuns who had been Mother Marie's favorites. They dared not attack her to Mother Marie, but they missed few opportunities to slight her in private. Thérèse saw all this and minded it, not for herself but because Carmel, which should have been the home of love, was failing in its vocation. Thérèse's sisters saw it, too, and resented it on her behalf, so that Thérèse had to work hard to persuade them to say nothing. When she told Sister Marie of the Trinity that she should be "grateful to the ones who are bent on keeping you from slowing down," she knew what she was talking about.

After Christmas, Thérèse wrote again to the Abbé Bellière to help him in his struggle to face the separation from his family: "You ask for comfort from the person Jesus has given you as sister—you have the right to do so. Since our Reverend Mother allowed me to write to you, I will try to fulfill the pleasant task that I have been given, but I think a more certain way of arriving at my goal is by praying and suffering."

She did not have to search for suffering that winter. The long days of prayer and work stretched unbearably ahead. In choir she tried to pray, battling against sleep, holding on to the edge of the stall to stop herself from falling. To stand up when it was her turn to chant needed such a violent effort that it left her sweating and giddy. There was no comfort even in prayer. She worked in the sacristy and did her share of the washing, which was now such a burden. She painted little cards, wrote pretty verses when they asked her to, and was patient and cheerful always. More and more often now, older nuns as well as novices came to her for help and advice, and some who had begun by despising or resenting her ended by admiring her wholeheartedly. To each one who came, she gave all she had of good sense, tact, and love.

Day after day she forced herself to go through the routine of the convent without complaint, and she succeeded so well that no one guessed there was anything seriously wrong with her. She shivered and sweated by turns as her temperature went up every evening, and the fever did odd things to her looks.

"How terribly ill you look!" said one Sister, seeing Thérèse, gray and exhausted, dragging herself along the passage from the choir one evening. "I am sure you are not long for this world, Sister!" But by the time she reached the community room, the fever had made her cheeks burn and her eyes very bright.

"How well you look, Sister!" said another nun who saw

her. "Quite radiant!" Thérèse smiled to herself, an ironic little smile.

She warmed herself for a few moments by the tiny fire (only a few moments; more would have been self-indulgence) before it was time to go to her cell.

Very slowly she began the long journey to the dormitory where her cell was. In her weakness she fell behind, so she was not noticed as she climbed the stairs, clinging to the handrail. She stopped on each step, leaning against the wall while she waited for her breathing to ease a little before tackling the next one. She reached her cell at last, her dear cell where she had suffered so much. But she still had to undress. That meant taking out the pins of her veil and scapular, and her arms felt as if they were loaded with lead weights. Sitting on her bed, she set about her task, stopping to rest between each movement. Her chilblained hands fumbled clumsily at the coarse serge, her fingers had no strength in them, she dropped things, and then there was the terrible effort of picking them up again. At each move her body was covered in sweat, but at last it was done. It had taken her an hour to undress—it did every night—and, of course, it would get worse.

She climbed painfully onto the hard bed and pulled at the worn blankets that did not keep out the cold. When she was lying down, the cough got worse. Her thin body shook with wrenching jerks as the bouts of coughing seized her, sending stabs of pain into her chest and throat. She feared that it might keep the others awake, so as she dozed fitfully through the dead hours of early morning, whenever the cough caught at her she buried her face in the pillow and stifled the noise with her handkerchief.

At this time little Sister Marie of the Trinity was assistant infirmarian. She knew that nothing would make Thérèse admit her illness as long as she could stand, but she could not bear to watch her suffering, and finally she went to the

Prioress to ask whether Thérèse could not be dispensed from going to Matins, the last Office of the day.

Mother Marie was short with her. "I have never heard before of young people like this, who think of nothing but their health!" she said. "In the old days, one would never have dreamed of missing Matins! If Sister Thérèse of the Child Jesus has reached the end of her strength, let her come and tell me so herself." And that Thérèse would not do. Perhaps she was wrong; it would have been more sensible to admit her illness and try to cure it, but she did not see it like that.

So Thérèse went on with her normal work and even did more. As the winter gave way to spring and she became weaker every day, she was working once more in the sacristy after a gap of a few months. Not content with that, on her days off duty, when all her work was done, she would dawdle past the sacristy so as to be within call if the first sacristan needed help, and this Sister always did find some jobs for her. Céline saw Thérèse and knew how much it must cost her, so she used to make signs to her to keep out of the sacristan's way, but obstinate as ever, Thérèse smiled and took no notice.

As Lent began once more, Thérèse faced the strict fast with a courage and cheerfulness that never faltered. She could scarcely drag herself about the convent and could no longer digest her food, then she began to spit blood as she had done the year before. The Prioress sent her to see the doctor again. This time even Dr. de Cornières, who was clearly not very clever, recognized what was called "consumption"—tuberculosis of the lungs. But he was undisturbed and quite resigned to his own powerlessness. "I shall not be able to cure her," he said sadly to the Prioress afterward. "Besides, her soul is not made for this earth!" But he decided to try some old treatments. Sister Thérèse was to be treated by hot poultices and by cauterizing her spine with a red-hot needle. These agonizing "treatments" did no good at all, so the doctor ordered more and more of them. Each time that this was done, Thérèse had to lie quietly in her cell for some hours, and indeed the pain was so awful that she would have found it difficult to walk.

Her cell overlooked the kitchen, and she lay there often during recreation, faint and sick with pain, while the infirmarian sat beside her. The chatter of the kitchen Sisters filtered through the shutters, breaking the silence of the little white room. "Sister Thérèse of the Child Jesus is going to die," sounded a cheerful voice above the clatter of the dishes. "I can't help wondering what our dear Mother will find to say about her after she is dead. She will be in a fix, because although the little Sister is very nice, I am sure she's done nothing worth talking about."

The infirmarian glanced at her patient and saw that she had heard every word. She could not help wondering whether Thérèse minded. "If you minded what people thought of you, you would certainly be disappointed today," she said half-seriously.

Thérèse shook her head a little. "What other people think?" she said. "Well, fortunately, God has always given me the grace not to care about that at all."

Yet she was as cheerful as a sparrow on the roof, so that many people still believed she was not ill. Certainly Father Roulland in China could not have guessed from her letters that there was anything wrong with her. He sent her his visiting card, printed in Chinese characters, and an account of his Chinese cook. Mother Marie Gonzaga allowed Thérèse to write back, although letters were usually forbidden during Lent.

"Your visiting card amused me very much," she wrote in a writing that was getting less neat and precise than it had been. "I do not even know which way round to hold it!"

She told him anything amusing that happened in the

convent, and once she described with delight how a live lobster escaped onto the kitchen floor and jumped about, refusing to be caught, so that the poor Sister cook declared the devil had got into him. "We laughed till we cried," wrote Thérèse.

Outside in the garden the chestnut trees that Thérèse loved so much were beginning to put out new furls of little leaves that gradually unwound and stretched out their pale green fans to the spring sunshine. The infirmarian thought it would do her patient good to walk in the garden for a while each day, and Thérèse obeyed. Painfully she dragged herself down the paths, moving slowly from one patch of sunlight to another. Thérèse's sister, Marie of the Sacred Heart, watched her one afternoon. After a few moments she went up to her and laid a hand on her arm. "Sister," she said with tender anxiety, "in your condition, walking can't do you any good—it only tires you more, that's all."

"I know." Thérèse smiled gratefully. "But do you know what gives me strength? Well, I walk for a missionary. I remember that in some faraway country, perhaps one of them is worn out by his work as an apostle, so to make his fatigues less I offer mine to God." Perhaps she was thinking of Father Roulland in China and hoping that the story about the lobster would make him laugh.

In the garden there were small oratories, each dedicated to a saint, which the nuns called "hermitages," and in the evening the community often met near one of these and sang a hymn. Still doing her best to live the ordinary life of the convent, Thérèse came, too, but the short walk from the house tired her so much that she had to sit down at once. The high voices rang out in the evening silence, but one of the nuns noticed that Thérèse was not standing up like the rest. She frowned and made a sign to her to get up. Thérèse saw her and with a terrific effort got to her feet once more. She could not sing, but she managed, somehow, to remain standing until the end of the hymn. Naturally, those who thought Thérèse's illness was not as bad as she made out found their suspicions confirmed by this. But the Prioress had realized at last that her dearest daughter was mortally ill and could no longer carry on as usual. This strange woman who could be so harsh now did all she could to comfort Thérèse. She gave permission to her three sisters to be with her a great deal. Sister Marie was allowed to cook her special food, Sister Geneviève helped to nurse her, and Mother Agnes was constantly with her in her cell, for in May the Prioress told Thérèse that she must give up her duties in the sacristy and linen room. Mother Agnes came to visit her sister in her cell the day after this, wondering whether it had been a great disappointment to her. Thérèse's eyes twinkled ironically at her serious sister. "At least now my death won't cause the slightest inconvenience to the community!"

"But don't you feel sad at appearing useless to the other Sisters?"

Thérèse thought of the blackness in which her soul was still buried and shook her head. "No, that is the least of my worries," she said shortly. Her bed was covered with little cards she had been painting, and the table beside her held her paints and brushes and a stack of cut pieces of vellum.

Mother Agnes glanced at the array of work and at the white, drawn face of her sister. "You never seem to be idle, even though you are ill," she said admiringly.

"I need to have some work on hand all the time, so that I don't have time to worry—and don't waste my time," replied Thérèse. She did not like praise.

One or another of the sisters visited her nearly every day, but the rest of the time she was alone, except when she had to endure more of Dr. de Cornières' "treatments." She could no longer see her novices regularly and could console herself and them only by sending them tiny notes and pictures.

Toward the end of May, she suddenly seemed much happier. The dark cloud lifted for a while from her soul.

The gossip of the community passed on to her by her sisters did not disturb her, and Mother Agnes—whose piety was always stronger than her understanding—liked to tell her things that were said about her. Mother Agnes was more and more convinced of her sister's holiness, and she hoped Thérèse would make a reply that would be worth remembering. "Someone said that you will be afraid of death," she said tactlessly one day.

"It's quite possible," answered Thérèse cheerfully. "If they only knew how little I depend on myself! I never depend much on my own thoughts. I know quite well how weak I am, but I can be glad of the feelings God gives me now. There will be time enough to put up with the opposite later."

Mother Agnes pulled a bundle of papers from the pocket under her scapular and sorted one out. "Here's one of the photographs of you that we took last year," she said, putting on her glasses, and she held out the little print to her sister. "It's quite good, isn't it?"

Thérèse looked. "Yes," she said, "but that's the envelope. When shall we see the letter? Oh, I would like to see the letter!"

20. *In Sight of Home*

THE DAYS dragged by. It did seem such a long time. "I know I'm going to die soon—but when? I can't tell. I am like a child that's always promised a cake—he sees it far off, then when he goes near to take it, the hand draws back! But I am perfectly prepared to live or die. I should be glad to be well and go to Cochin China if God wanted it."

"The doctor is doing his best to cure you," said Mother Agnes hopefully.

"Yes," agreed Thérèse, "and at first I was upset at taking such expensive medicines, but now it doesn't bother me at all. I read that St. Gertrude was glad to think that things like that could at least be a gain to the person who gave them. I know quite well that all these remedies are perfectly useless," Thérèse said, smiling at her sister, "but I have made arrangements with God that they shall go to help the poor missionaries who have not time or money to take care of themselves. I have asked him to use all the care given to me to cure them instead."

Mother Agnes was moved. "You are very brave," she said, "and other people think so, too."

But Thérèse refused to let the conversation become too solemn. "People often say I am brave," she admitted, "but I say to myself, 'It isn't strictly true—only it would never do to let everyone be cheated!' So I set myself to get some courage with the help of grace. I am just like a soldier who has been congratulated on his bravery, when he knows quite well he is really a coward—in the end he is shamed by the compliments into trying to deserve them."

Mother Agnes and several other nuns who realized how ill she was wanted to move her to the infirmary. "You would be much more comfortable there," they said.

But Thérèse was distressed. "I would much rather stay in my cell than go down to the infirmary," she protested, trying for once to get her own way. "Here no one hears me coughing and I don't disturb anyone. Besides, when I'm too well looked after, I'm not happy any more."

Another of Mother Agnes's ideas worried Thérèse very much. Her elder sister wanted to preserve every possible reminder of her—even her words. So she got a little notebook, and whenever Thérèse said something she thought interesting, she wrote it down at once. Thérèse did not like it; she always distrusted anything that was not straightforward and simple. It all seemed a bit artificial, and it embarrassed her to see that little book and pencil come out whenever she opened her mouth. But she gave in because she saw how much it meant to her sister, and she could not bear to hurt her feelings. Her own feelings, of course, she did not consider. Thanks to Mother Agnes's rather strange devotion, a great many of the things Thérèse said in her last months are recorded which would otherwise have been lost. Thérèse sacrificed her own feelings for the sake of her sister; but without knowing it, she was making a present to the whole world.

Her devoted sister did not stop at that. She still treasured the story of Thérèse's childhood and vocation, which her sister had written at her orders and delivered to her on January 21, 1896. The long "letter" that Thérèse had also written, at her sister Marie's request, contained a great deal about Thérèse's way of living and thinking, but not the actual story of her life as a Carmelite. Mother Agnes had never told the present Prioress, Mother Marie Gonzaga, about the original story, but time was getting short, and she decided to risk a snub. She went to the Prioress after Matins and Lauds on June 2, 1897. "Mother," she said, "I can't go to sleep without having told you a secret. When I was Prioress, Sister Thérèse, in order to please me and under obedience, wrote down some recollections of childhood. I reread them the other day. They are charming, but you won't find much in them to help you compose the obituary to send to the other Carmels after her death, because there is little in them about her life as a nun. If you were to tell her to, she could write something more valuable, and I don't doubt that you would have something incomparably better than I have."

Mother Agnes knew how to appeal to the Prioress. Next morning, Mother Marie ordered Thérèse to go on with her story, and Thérèse was given another cheap exercise book, a small black one this time, and a pen. In the warm summer weather, she was wheeled out into the garden in an invalid chair. Under the shadow of the chestnut trees, she opened the book and wrote, taking up the tale where she had left it off.

"We must economize and write between the lines," she said to Mother Agnes. But her sister would not let her—it was too exhausting. Slowly, steadily, the pages were covered with writing that was a little less neat but still firm. Thérèse wrote to the Prioress, whom she loved. She wrote to thank her for the severity that had braced her, for the humiliations that had indeed brought her low, so low she no longer mattered to herself, for only God mattered. She wrote of her "way," the way of spiritual childhood, the way which was, she said, an elevator to Heaven for little souls too weak to climb the stairs.

Around her the nuns worked in the garden, weeding, watering, tidying, and every now and then one or another came up to talk to Thérèse, to bring her flowers or just to gossip. Mother Agnes watched Thérèse put down her pen to greet each Sister with a welcoming smile. She never gave the least sign of annoyance at the interruption.

"Poor little Sister, it must tire you terribly to write all day!" said one sympathetically.

"Don't worry!" answered Thérèse with patient irony. "I seem to write a lot, but really I write almost nothing!"

"That's good," replied the other, reassured. "But all the same, I'm glad we're all gardening; it must give you a little amusement."

"How can you be so patient when you are constantly interrupted?" asked her sister.

Thérèse laughed. "I am writing about brotherly love," she said, "so it is a good chance to practice it!" But in the end she got out a book and said she was copying out bits of the Psalms and the Gospels for the Prioress's feast. She thought it might keep the Sisters away.

During those days at the beginning of June, the shadow was still lifted from her; she was radiant. She thought she would die soon, and one evening when her three sisters came to see her, she said good-bye to them. "I am so happy, little sisters," she said. "I think I am going to die soon—I am sure of it. But don't be surprised if I don't appear to you after my death and if you don't get any extraordinary sign of my happiness—you must remember that it is in the spirit of my "little way" *not* to wish to see anything. Don't worry if I suffer a great deal and if you see no sign of happiness at the moment of my death—Our Lord really died as a Victim of love, and you know how great *his* agony was."

But Thérèse did not die then. She still took her walks

in the garden, leaning on the arm of one of her sisters. The weather was wonderful, and the Prioress decided to take the opportunity to get a good photograph of Thérèse, for there might not be another chance. Céline—Sister Geneviève —was the photographer, and she arranged the elaborate affair. She chose an ivy-covered wall near the infirmary window as a background, and they all thought it would be a good idea if Thérèse were to hold pictures of the Holy Child and of the Holy Face of Jesus, because these were her titles in religion. She knelt down, holding up the two pictures, like Moses holding up the Tablets of the Law, and Céline arranged her veil, her scapular, the heavy folds of the white choir cloak that she wore for the occasion. It was very hot, and Thérèse had a temperature. She knelt quietly until everything was ready, and then held the pose rigidly for the nine seconds' exposure that was needed. Was it all over? Céline shook her head. She had to develop the plate to make sure that it was all right. While she waited, Thérèse could rest in the sunshine, glad that for these few days at least the lovely light of the sun seemed to find a home in her soul as well. She was at peace and very happy, although she had a feeling that it would not last.

Céline came back, looking disappointed. The plate was a failure; they would have to try again. Again Thérèse knelt, again they fussed over the folds of her habit. She smiled at her busy sister and tried to keep quite still, but she was terribly tired, and she moved without meaning to while the plate was being exposed. It all had to be done again. While they were getting everything arranged once more, Thérèse's endless patience cracked just a little. "Do hurry up," she begged. "I am so exhausted." But she was determined not to give way. She faced the camera as if it were a firing squad, and although she had no strength to smile, her face was serene. At last it was done. She could sit down and relax, as far as the pain in her side allowed.

Mother Agnes supported her as she walked slowly back through the garden. Her tired eyes noticed a little white hen scuttling down the path with her chicks. As the two nuns came near, the anxious mother summoned her babies and covered them with her white wings, defying all enemies to dare touch her rustling, cheeping brood. Suddenly, gentle tears began to run down Thérèse's face as she remembered how Our Lord had wanted to gather all his people together "as a hen gathers her chicks under her wings." To Mother Agnes's startled question, she explained with a smile, "I cried because God has given us that comparison in the Gospel so that we may understand his tenderness. All my life he has done that for me; he has covered me entirely with his wings. The feeling was too strong for me—it was more than I could keep in my heart—but I only cried from love and thankfulness."

The days of light and happiness in her soul continued as her body grew weaker and weaker. June 9, 1897, was the second anniversary of her offering of herself to the love of God, and she was full of joy on that day, though so ill that she could not stand up alone. Her two elder sisters came to see her after recreation.

"They say you are getting better," said Mother Agnes.

Thérèse was not interested. "Last week, when I could stand up, they thought I was very ill. This week when I am so exhausted that I cannot hold myself upright, they think I am saved! But what does it matter *what* they say?"

"Do you think you will die soon all the same?"

"Yes, I expect I shall go quite soon. I am certainly not getting better. My side aches very much."

Sister Marie could not bear it. Thérèse's matter-of-fact way of talking about her death could not hide from her the fact that her darling sister was going to leave her. "What a desert life there will be for us when you're dead!" she blurted out suddenly.

Thérèse looked at her sister strangely, and when she spoke it was in a voice they had never heard before, almost as if she were repeating something she had been told. "Oh, no," she said slowly, "you will see it will be like a shower of roses. Yes, I shall send down a shower of roses."

There was silence in the little cell for a few minutes, no sound but the summer noises from the garden, noises of birds, busy footsteps, the warm hum of bees and flies.

Then Thérèse broke the spell with a little laugh. "I am like a small child waiting at the railway station for his mother and father to put him in a train. But, oh, dear—they don't come, and the train leaves!" She gave a quick little sigh, then smiled again. "But there are other trains, and I shan't miss them all."

During those lovely days, she could see clearly in the distance "the lighthouse which showed me the harbor of Heaven," as she said. Then suddenly the light went out. She was once more in darkness, which seemed worse than ever after the bright days, and with the darkness came the voices of evil, tempting her to doubt.

She sat in the garden in the wheelchair, slowly writing line after line, as the Prioress had asked her to do. She wrote with a pencil now, because it was too difficult to dip the pen in the ink. More and more slowly she wrote. She tried to describe at last what she suffered in that darkness of soul: "When, weary of being enveloped by nothing but shadows, I try to comfort and encourage myself with the thought of the radiant country for which I long, it only doubles my torment. The darkness seems to borrow the voices of sinners and mock me: 'You dream of light and of a fragrant land; you dream that the Creator of this loveliness will be your own for all eternity; you dream of escaping one day from the mists which surround you! Go on! Go on! Welcome death, which will bring you not what you hope for but an even darker night, the night of nothingness!'

"Dearest Mother, this picture that I've tried to give of the darkness that shadows my soul is as imperfect as a sketch compared with the model, but I dare not say more for fear it might be blasphemy. I'm afraid I have said too much already. May Jesus forgive me if I have hurt him, but he knows that I try to practice my faith even though it brings me no joy. I have made more acts of faith in one year than during all the rest of my life."

But she was still as cheerful as ever and refused to let her sisters be gloomy either. She wrote to Maurice Bellière as well, to cheer him up and encourage him, for he was very worried about his past sins: "Remembering my own faults humbles me and teaches me never to rely on my own strength, which is mere weakness; but even more, this memory of them teaches me about mercy and love. If, with the trust of a child, we cast our faults into the furnace of love, don't you think they will be burnt up, never to return?"

Day after day she worked at the story of God's dealings with her soul; she wrote about the novices and how he had always shown her how to deal with them; she wrote about the suffering and death which lay ahead and, chiefly, of the love which made it all worthwhile.

But she could not go on for long. Even a pencil became too heavy for her thin fingers to hold; the effort of writing exhausted her, and she had to give in. At the beginning of July, she gave to the Prioress the pages she had managed to write.

On July 4 she began to bring up blood again, so that everyone thought she would die any minute. Poor Thérèse hoped so herself, but Mother Agnes prayed desperately for her sister's cure. She lit a little lamp in front of Our Lady's statue, to beg her prayers that at least the hemorrhages should stop.

But Thérèse could not understand her attitude. "Aren't you pleased that I am dying?" she said. "As for me, I am delighted to go on bringing up blood. But it's stopped for today," she added regretfully. It came again, and she began to hope. "I shall go to see God very soon!" she gasped joyfully when the bleeding stopped, and Mother Agnes was torn between admiration and grief.

"Aren't you afraid of death now that it seems so near?" she asked gently.

"Less and less," answered her sister, smiling.

They had sent for the doctor at last, and while they waited, Mother Agnes and the infirmarian tidied the bed and got the patient ready. Mother Agnes thought it would be lovely if Thérèse said something holy to the doctor, but when she suggested it, Thérèse came as near to giving her a direct snub as her love for her "little mother" would allow. "But, Mother, that is not my way of doing things at all!" she protested. "Let Dr. de Cornières think whatever he likes. I like nothing better than straightforwardness, and I hate the opposite. I tell you that to do as you ask would suit me very ill!"

Dr. de Cornières came and was grave and fussy and did nothing—there was really nothing he could do. Thérèse smiled and thanked him. By the next day she was so ill that at last she was forced to give in to her sisters' wishes and go to the infirmary.

Her sisters came to carry her down from her cell. At the door she turned to look once more at the whitewashed walls, the scrubbed floor, the hard bed, the bench and stool, the little lamp with the wick one had to push up with a pin, the chipped jug and bowl on the floor. These things had been her only companions in long hours of pain as well as in days and years of happiness. "When I am in Heaven you must remember that a great part of my happiness was won in this little cell," she said, "for I have suffered a lot here. I would have liked to die here."

Down the stairs they went, very slowly—stairs that she had

swept when she was a postulant, stairs that had taken her
so long to climb all through that last, long winter. They
passed down the cloister, and she could see the quadrangle
with its beds of roses showing between the arches. There
stood the great stone crucifix beside which she had posed
to be photographed when she was a novice. They turned
through the door of the infirmary—one of the several rooms
for the sick.

Beside the bed stood the statue of the Mother of Jesus that
had seemed to come alive for Thérèse that day when she
had been cured of her frightening illness. It had been
brought there from her home when the family left *Les
Buissonnets.* She paused to look at it, smiling happily.

Marie, watching her face, remembered that far-off day, too.
"What do you see, Sister?" she asked softly.

Thérèse knew what she was thinking about. "It has never
looked more beautiful to me," she said, "but today it is just
the statue. You know very well that before it wasn't the
statue."

As they helped her to take off her habit, she stretched
out her arms in front of her and laughed. "I am already a
skeleton!" she said, looking at her terribly thin wrists and
the hands whose pale skin seemed scarcely strong enough
to cover the fine bones. "That's something that really cheers
me up!"

They dressed her in her invalid's habit and helped her
into bed. She lay back exhausted on her pillows and looked
around her. The sunlight streamed in through the high
windows with their white curtains. It shone on the neat
metal bed draped with brown bed-curtains, and on the
few straight chairs; it was reflected back by the gleaming
waxed floor. This room, warm and light and peaceful, would
be her Calvary.

21. *The Royal Road*

"**I** REMEMBER I once got too much pleasure from using a bottle of eau de cologne when I was traveling," said Thérèse thoughtfully to Mother Agnes of Jesus. She was examining her conscience because she hoped soon to receive the last Anointing, and among the sins she might have committed through her senses, that was all she could think of.

Before she could receive the last Sacraments, the Superior of the convent had to be consulted. So on July 9, Thérèse had another visitor.

Across the polished floor strode Canon Delatröette, her old opponent who had later learned to admire her. But for all his admiration he had not changed much. "You!" he said jokingly, looking down at the face on the pillow. "Setting off for Heaven so soon! You haven't made your crown yet--you've only just begun!" (At fifteen he had thought her too young to be a Carmelite; now perhaps he thought that at twenty-four she was too young to die.)

But Thérèse agreed with him. "What you say is quite true. No, I have not made my crown yet!" She smiled up at him. "But God has made it for me!" And as he sat beside her and talked, she never gave any hint of what she was suffering, but was as gay and cheerful as usual. Canon Delatröette decided that no one who smiled and chatted like that could be at death's door; certainly there was no need for the last Sacraments yet.

At last he left, and Mother Agnes turned to her sister. "You don't know how to get what you want," she said a little reproachfully.

Thérèse twinkled. "I don't know the tricks of the trade!" she answered.

The days and nights passed with terrible slowness. She told them, "God will do all I want in Heaven, because on earth I have never done my own will."

"You will look down on us from Heaven, won't you?" asked one of them.

"No," she answered radiantly. "I shall *come* down."

All the time the astonishing thing about her was that she looked so happy. It was not a pretense; she really was happy, with a deep, peaceful happiness that nothing could shake, because it was founded on love stronger than death. Beside that love, suffering seemed rather unimportant, even the worst of all her sufferings—the feeling of being abandoned by God. Or, rather, her suffering was another reason for happiness, because it made her more like Jesus. She wanted no less of it; but, however many days she might drag on, she knew that her strength was running out, and during July she made great efforts to write to all the people she loved.

She wrote to Maurice Bellière, telling him bluntly: "Perhaps when you read this little note, I shan't be on earth any more but in the heart of eternal joy! I do not know the future, but all the same I can tell you for certain that the Bridegroom is at the door. It would take a miracle to hold me longer in exile, and I do not imagine that Jesus would work a useless miracle." But she was happy to die, she told him, and he was not to think that she would stop helping him. "By prayer my soul will always be with you, and your faith will give you a sense of the presence of the little sister that Jesus has given you to help you, not just for barely two years but until the very last evening of your life."

She wrote to Father Roulland, thanking him for his last letter. He was learning Chinese and said he felt like a baby learning to talk. "Well, I am a baby, too," she wrote. "For the past five or six weeks, I have been living on mush, but soon I shall sit down at the heavenly banquet and quench my thirst with the waters of eternal life!" To this brother also she promised her help. "I feel sure that I shall be much more useful in Heaven than on earth, so I announce to you with joy that I shall soon enter the city of the blessed, and I am sure you will share my joy and thank the Lord for giving me the chance to help you more efficiently in your apostolic work. You see, brother, that if I am already leaving the battlefield, it is not from a selfish desire to rest. The thought of eternal happiness scarcely moves me, because for a long time, suffering has been my Heaven on earth, and I find it difficult to imagine how I shall get used to a country where joy reigns without any trace of sadness! Jesus will have to change my soul and make it able to appreciate joy, otherwise I should not be able to bear eternal happiness. What attracts me to the Kingdom of Heaven is the Lord's call, the hope of being able to love him at last as much as I have always wanted to, and the thought that I shall be able to make him loved by a multitude of souls who will bless him forever."

The novices were much in her thoughts and also Sister

Marie of the Trinity, who was giving trouble again. She had been assistant infirmarian, but when Thérèse was admitted to the infirmary, Sister Marie was sent to other work because of possible infection. She took this as a slight and complained loudly about it, and her words were repeated to Thérèse. In spite of her exhaustion, Thérèse found strength to write her a stern little note: "I am sorry for your weakness—why *must* you say always what you think *at once?* I do not want you to be sad. You know I dream of high perfection for you—that is why I speak to you severely. I would have understood your struggles and comforted you gently if you had not spoken it all aloud. Good-bye, my poor child. I shall have to take you to Heaven in a hurry!"

One morning stood out for her—the feast of Our Lady of Mount Carmel. She had been less sick and was allowed to receive communion. A young priest was celebrating his first Mass, and afterward he carried the host down the cloisters, spread with flowers to welcome the King. The infirmary was decorated like a shrine for the great feast. As the priest carried the Blessed Sacrament into the room, the clear boyish voice of Sister Marie of the Eucharist rang out, singing one of Thérèse's own songs.

Later, Thérèse wrote for the last time to her uncle and aunt, thanking them for all their care of her when she was a child, and she told them about the morning's communion, for she knew it would please them to have news of their daughter: "Before my communion she sang a little verse that I made up for this morning. When Jesus was in my heart she sang again that line from my poem: 'To live in love, to die of love is a sweet martyrdom.' I know my sisters have told you about my gaiety. It is true. I am just like a chaffinch except when I have a high temperature, but luckily that usually happens only at night, when finches sleep with their heads under their wings! But I would not be so gay if God did not show me that the only joy on earth is to do his will. One day I think I am at Heaven's gate because Dr. de Cornières looks so worried—and the next day, off he goes quite delighted, saying, 'Now you are getting better!' But I think to myself (although I am only a baby living on mush!) that I shan't get better, although I may drag on for a long time still."

Léonie needed a letter. Cut off from all her sisters and unable to see Thérèse, who was dying, she lived on with her uncle and aunt—a dreary and disappointing life. Thérèse put her finger on the trouble and pointed out the cure: "The only happiness on earth is to try to be delighted with the share God has given us. Yours is very lovely, my dearest sister. If you want to be a saint it will be easy for you, because in your heart the world counts for nothing. Just like us, you can be occupied with the 'one thing necessary.'"

Thérèse, too, was helpless and useless, but she knew it would not be for long. One night she turned to her sisters, her face glowing with hope. "I feel that my work is just going to begin," she said slowly, "my work of making souls love God as I love him, of teaching my little way to souls. If I get my wish, I shall spend my Heaven here on earth until the end of the world."

They listened, only half understanding, but she knew what she was saying. "Yes, I shall spend my Heaven in doing good on earth. It is not impossible, because the angels who have the vision of God are able to watch over us. I shall not be able to rest until the end of the world as long as there are any souls to be saved. But when the angel announces, 'Time is no more,' then I shall rest, then I shall be happy, because the number of the blessed will be complete, and all will have found their joy and rest. It's a thrilling idea!"

"Tell me about the way you want to teach," asked Mother Agnes.

"It's the way of spiritual childhood, Mother," she answered. "The way of trust, the complete giving up of one's

self. I want to show them the little ways that have succeeded
so well for me. I shall tell them there is only one thing to
be done on earth, and that is to scatter the flowers of small
sacrifices before Jesus and win him by tenderness. That is
what I have done, and that is why I shall be welcomed."

Thérèse spent a lot of time trying to cheer up people
who were sad about her. The Abbé Bellière got the letter
she had written on the thirteenth and was so upset that she
had to write again. In spite of her weakness, she wrote him
a long letter, showing him once more her way to Heaven,
by the way of suffering joined with love, going to God by
the "elevator" of love, not by the steep stairway of fear.
She promised to help him to understand this way better
after her death. "Please, dearest little brother, try to believe that instead of losing me you will *find* me and that I
will not leave you any more." And she enclosed one of the
photographs that Sister Geneviève had taken in June. "The
novices made a great fuss when they saw it, saying I had put
on my majestic look; apparently I am usually more smiling.
But, little brother, I promise you that if my photograph
does not smile at you, at least my soul will never stop smiling
for you, for I shall be near you."

But even that was not enough. He wrote back, much
cheered, and Thérèse was glad. But he was still worrying
about his sins, just as she had done, and again she tried to
lift him up, to show him her own way to God, the simple
way of a child who trusts its father. To help him she told
him in a few pages the story of her own childhood. She
wrote about her parents, about her father's terrible illness,
and of how at last the four sisters all came to Carmel. She
wrote in pencil, in short snatches, for her strength quickly
gave out. Still, for love of poverty, she tried to squeeze in
as much as possible on each page.

It was becoming more and more difficult to write, and
most of her time was taken up simply by being ill. She did

not forget her Sisters though. On washday she thought of them all toiling in the sweltering heat of the washhouse. The Sisters are very tired with their washing, she thought. O God, comfort them all, and let the work be done in peace and love. Lying in bed, she could at least have the joy of sharing in their discomfort.

Toward the end of July, she was so much worse that it was decided to let her have the last Sacraments. Through the hot midday hours, she prayed, trying to prepare herself.

The air shimmered in the heat, and flies buzzed around her face. Patiently she brushed away the noisy insects but would not kill them. "They are my only enemies," she managed to smile, "and God tells us to forgive our enemies."

In the afternoon the Superior came to see her, hear her confession, and talk to her about the Anointing. "You will be like a little child who has just been baptized," he told her.

The infirmary was polished until every corner shone. The little table beside Thérèse's bed was covered with a white cloth. On it stood a big crucifix, and on each side of that a candle whose little flame glimmered palely in the sunlight. A glass of water and another vessel with holy water caught the sun, sparkling and shimmering and making tiny rainbows on the smooth linen. Flowers filled every part of the room with their crisp, living colors and cool scent. The bedclothes had been smoothed until no wrinkle dared to remain, and the slight shape under the blankets did not disturb them. Between the dark bed-curtains, she lay against her pillows, her face almost as white as the linen, her eyes watching the door expectantly.

At last the priest came. *"Pax huic domui,"* he said. "Peace be to this house." And coming forward into the hushed room, he stood by the bed and sprinkled it with holy water. "Sprinkle me with hyssop, Lord, and I shall be cleansed. Wash me, and I shall be whiter than snow."

He gave communion to Thérèse. "Sister," he said, "receive the journey money of the Body of Our Lord, Jesus Christ, that he may protect thee from the malicious enemy and bring thee safe to everlasting life." (Her journey would be longer and more terrible than he knew, but she had said, "Jesus will have to pay my fare!")

After the priest had dipped his fingers in the water, Thérèse drank it so that no smallest particle of the host should be lost. Her eyes were lowered, her hands lay on the sheet like two little dead birds. All around the Sisters prayed for her.

From far away came the noises of the town, the rumble of wheels on the stones, a horse's hooves going slowly in the heat, people walking, a door slamming in the street, a train rattling through the station.

The warm murmur of a garden in summer drifted in through the open window, leaves brushed and rustled as a breeze passed, bees hummed.

Sometimes in the quiet room a stifled sigh broke the hush, the click of a rosary, the rustle of a woollen habit against the boards as someone shifted slightly.

Over the little sounds rose the voice of the priest reading the Latin prayers, bidding the evil spirit go, asking God to send his angels into that place, bringing his gifts of peace, joy, and everlasting health.

He made the sign of the cross over the still figure in the bed. "Be there quenched in thee all power of Satan through the laying on of my hands and by calling upon all the Holy Angels, Archangels, Prophets, Apostles, Martyrs, Confessors, Virgins, and all the Saints together. Amen."

Open on the table lay a tiny silver box of sweet ointment, the oil for the sick. The priest dipped his thumb in it and bent over the bed. Gently he touched the closed eyelids with the oil in the form of a cross. "Through this holy Anointing and through his most tender mercy, may the Lord forgive thee whatsoever thou hast done wrong through sight."

The Sacrament of the sick brought, under the sign of Anointing, the prayers of the Church that the one who was cut off by illness might be given back to life and health. But, as in the Gospels Christ both healed and forgave in one gesture of love, the Sacrament of healing is for health of body and spirit. It brings Christ's love to help the weakness and fearfulness of the sick who might doubt the mercy of God.

Very gently the priest anointed all the inlets of the senses. On ears and nostrils and lips he signed the sign of salvation, and on the hands and feet.

"Lord have mercy."

"Christ have mercy."

"Lord have mercy."

Then the Lord's Prayer.

"Save your servant, O Lord," said the priest.

"Whose hope is in you, my God," came the answer. The responses swung to and fro.

The Church called upon the Lord to help his servant, to defend her against the evil one, to soothe and heal and forgive.

When it was over, Thérèse lay still in deep and happy silence, her mind full of thankfulness.

After a moment, she stretched out to her sisters her hands, still faintly glistening with the oil. She looked at them with reverence, for they were like a priest's hands, which are anointed with oil at his ordination, when he is chosen to offer the sacrifice of thanksgiving—the Eucharist—for God's people. Her sacrifice was herself.

But she was allowed no peace in which to thank God for what he had done for her. Almost as soon as the priest had gone, the nuns came crowding back to see her. Would she die at once? Would she get better now? Would she look ecstatic like a saint? Would she say something thrilling or have a vision? They came because they loved her; they did not mean to be unkind, but their thoughtlessness gave her no peace on this day when, above all, she longed to be left alone. For each Sister she had a welcoming smile and a word of thanks, and when Mother Agnes sympathized with her, "I thought of how Our Lord was followed by the crowds when he wanted to go away by himself," explained Thérèse, "so I wanted to imitate him by welcoming my Sisters kindly."

They were all expecting her to die any minute. Someone in a hurry left the door to the next infirmary open, and Thérèse caught sight of the straw mattress that had been brought down from her cell to receive her dead body, as was the custom. She laughed suddenly. "There's my palliasse," she said. "It's quite ready for my body." And she made them laugh by describing her funeral as if it were all a huge joke.

But the palliasse would not be needed yet. She got no better, but "dragged on," as she had expected, from day to day.

Sister Geneviève was made assistant infirmarian and never left her except to snatch a little sleep in the cell next door or to go to Office. Mother Agnes or Sister Marie of the Sacred Heart watched by her at those times, and Mother Agnes went on carefully writing down everything the girl said, with slight alterations sometimes, to make the words seem more obviously "holy."

One warm afternoon all three sisters sat beside the bed. Thérèse seemed to be dozing, and the room was very still. The heads of the three watchers, weary from broken nights, began to nod drowsily in the heat. Thérèse was not asleep, but pain left her no energy to spare for talk. Tenderly she looked at her sleepy sisters, and she smiled, remembering how the three disciples had slept from weariness while their Master sweated blood in Gethsemane. A faint sound somewhere in the convent made the sleepers start up to see Thérèse gazing at them with her gently amused smile. "Peter, James, John," she said, pointing to each in turn.

Mother Agnes talked to her about her story. More and more, Thérèse seemed to realize that what she had written was very important. She insisted that it must be published as soon as she was dead, she who a year before had not cared even if it were burned. "If you don't publish at once, the devil will try several tricks to prevent or spoil God's work, and it is *very important work.*"

Mother Agnes felt that some of the manuscript might need altering, so she asked Thérèse to read it through. As she read, the easy tears of weakness ran down her face.

"What's the matter?" asked Mother Agnes anxiously.

"What I have been reading over in my manuscript—it shows so well what I'm like. Mother, these pages will do a great deal of good, they will make God's loving-kindness better known. I am sure the world will come to love me."

She spoke as if she were talking about someone else. There was no self-love left in her at all, so that she talked about herself simply as God's instrument, which he would use for great things. But before she became a perfect instrument, she had more to endure.

During the night of August 6, the Feast of the Transfiguration, they hung up a picture of the Holy Face by her bed with flowers and a night-light.

All through the night she struggled against the worst temptations to doubt God's goodness that she had yet known, making one act of faith after another, clinging with her eyes to the suffering face of Jesus, lit from below by the tiny flame. In the morning she was exhausted but triumphant.

22. *The Gates of Heaven*

Aʟʟ ᴛʜʀᴏᴜɢʜ August the pain got worse, but Dr. de Cornières was away for a holiday. His substitute was Thérèse's cousin by marriage, François la Néèle, and he told the Prioress that the patient was in such a serious state that she ought to see a doctor every day. But Mother Marie Gonzaga disapproved of too much fuss over illness, feeling perhaps, with another of her changes of mood, that a Carmelite should keep going to the end. During that month she let the doctor come only three times.

Thérèse wrote one last time to her little brother, Maurice Bellière. "I am all ready to go," she wrote. "I have been given my passport for Heaven!" He was afraid that she would be less able to excuse his faults when she was in Heaven with the God of Justice. "Have you forgotten that I shall also share in the endless mercy of the Lord?" she asked him. She would also leave him some little things as souvenirs; the Prioress had allowed her to. One of them was a little crucifix, the first one she had had. "It is not beautiful, the face of Christ has almost disappeared, but you will not be surprised when I tell you that this souvenir of one of my sisters has been everywhere with me since I was thirteen." He had been given the part of St. Louis in a play at the seminary. "I congratulate you on your new honor," she wrote. "On the 25th, the day I keep my dear Father's feast, I shall also have the joy of remembering Brother Louis of France! Good-bye, may God give us the grace to love him and to save souls for him—that is the wish of your unworthy little sister, Thérèse of the Child Jesus and of the Holy Face."

The next day she managed to write a tiny note of fare-well to Léonie, thanking her for a little bedcover she had made for the sister she was not able to see. She would offer her communion the next day for her. "I love you and I kiss you," she ended.

But soon she could no longer receive communion, be-cause she was sick so often. She made her last communion on August 19 and offered it for the salvation of a priest who had left the Church. She was so weak that she fainted while the nuns were singing the psalm "Miserere" before com-munion. Afterward one of the Sisters put a crucifix into Thérèse's hands. She looked at it for a long time and kissed the thorn-pierced head, which was bent down to one side. "He's dead. I like it better when he's shown dead, because then I think that he isn't suffering any more." But Thérèse's own sufferings were by no means over, and being deprived of communion was not the least of them.

The remedies they tried made things worse—not only the painful poultices and disgusting medicines, but more or-dinary things that she happened to dislike very much. She hated milk, and the doctor had ordered a milk diet. She, who suffered patiently the most intense agony, found a glass of milk almost more than she could bear.

"Would you drink it to save my life?" asked Mother Agnes teasingly.

"Oh yes," she answered, horrified. "And I won't do it for the love of God!" Ashamed, she took the glass and drank it straight off. It was the same with other things. Like most people, she found many things in her nursing and treatment embarrassing and humiliating, but she made herself be sensible about them, and her sense of humor helped.

When the pain lessened for a little while, she talked to the novices, advising and helping them with all the energy she could gather and even being severe when necessary. One of her visitors was the tearful novice who had been cured by making her catch her tears in a shell. The poor girl came now to ask Thérèse whether she might, please, cry when her dear mistress was dead. "Oh, yes," said Thérèse kindly, though her eyes twinkled with silent laughter, "but only into the shell!"

To her sisters she talked often about the Holy Family. She disliked fanciful stories about miracles that the Child Jesus did, when the lovely thing about the Holy Family was its ordinariness. She almost seemed to see the little group in their daily life at Nazareth. "The country women came to chat with the Blessed Virgin. Sometimes they asked her to let little Jesus go and play with their children, and Jesus looked at the Blessed Virgin to see if he could go." They listened enchanted.

On August 30 they carried her on a little bed out into the cloister near the infirmary to take a last photograph of her. As before, when Céline had made her kneel in the garden, they wanted to make her into a sort of holy picture, of the kind people liked. So they gave her a crucifix to hold, and some roses.

But soon a telegram brought Dr. la Néèle back from a visit to Caen, for she was much worse. He found it difficult to believe that she could be in such a state and still live.

Thérèse was in such agony that she knew that only her great faith in God's goodness kept her from going mad. The darkness in her soul increased, and she pointed one day to a shadowy grotto under the overhanging bushes and trees that she could see from the window. "Do you see that dark place down by the chestnut trees where you can't make anything out? I am in a place just like that, soul and body. Such darkness—but I am at peace there."

September came, the leaves began to turn yellow, the flowers the nuns brought to the infirmary were the big tawny blooms of autumn. One day, though, a Sister found a few violets flowering in a shady corner and brought them to her. She thought them lovely and breathed in their cool scent with delight, but only after Mother Agnes had re-assured her that it would not be self-indulgent to do so. The next day it was a fat, overblown rose. As she held it, the petals began to slip off onto the bed, and she picked them up slowly in tired fingers, touching with each petal the wounds of Christ on her crucifix. Some slipped from her feeble fingers and slid to the floor. "Gather up those petals carefully, little Sisters," she said. "They will be used to please people later on. Don't lose one of them."

Dr. de Cornières came back from his holiday and was horrified at his patient's condition. He told the Prioress she ought to be given injections of morphia to deaden the pain, but Mother Marie would not hear of it. She thought it shameful for a Carmelite to be helped in that way. She even objected to mild morphine syrup, which might have helped a little, but she grudgingly allowed doses of this, such small doses that they were nearly useless. Being strong her-self, she probably could not imagine the sort of pain that Thérèse was enduring.

As the month went on, the watchers in the sickroom marveled that she still lived and could hardly bear to see her suffering. Thérèse was as peaceful as ever. "I know for certain now that everything I've said and written is perfectly true—it's true that I've wanted to suffer a great deal for God, and it's true that I still want it."

"But what you are suffering is frightful," said one of them in horror.

Thérèse looked at her seriously, rather surprised. "No, it's not frightful," she said peacefully. "A little victim of love can never find what her Bridegroom sends 'frightful.'"

But the tide was running out at last. One night Sister Geneviève came into the infirmary and found Thérèse awake, with folded hands. "What are you doing?" she said reproachfully. "You should try to get a little sleep."

"I can't sleep, so I am praying."

"What are you saying to Jesus?"

"I am not saying anything to him—I just love him."

On September 29 she made her last confession. She made it to a priest she had not seen before. She was so weak that she could not lower her veil over her face as was usual, and he was able to look at her. He was astounded at her beauty. As a child Thérèse had been pretty, but now there was no prettiness left—only, in her thin, pale face, the radiance of peace. The infirmary seemed to him a sort of shrine for this lovely creature who scarcely belonged to the earth any more.

That day they thought the end had come, for a horrible rattling sounded in her chest. "Is this the agony, Mother?" she gasped to the Prioress. "How ought I to set about dying? I shall never know how to die!"

They read prayers for the dying, but the hours dragged on. The doctor came and went, and again she asked, "Is it today, Mother?"

"Yes," answered the Prioress, her harsh voice gentle and pitying. "God is very joyful today."

"So am I," cried Thérèse, but still she could not die.

All morning she struggled for breath. "I am utterly exhausted," she whispered at midday. "Pray for me—if you only knew!"

Evening came. Sister Geneviève sat with her as she lay in silent agony. In the twilight silence, about nine o'clock, there was a fluttering of wings, and they saw a little gray turtledove come and perch on the windowsill. It stood there for a long time cooing gently, and the two sisters remembered the words of the Song of Songs, words of the Bridegroom calling his bride: "Rise up, rise up quickly, dear heart, so gentle, so beautiful, rise up and come with me. Winter is now over, the rain has passed by. At home the flowers have begun to blossom, pruning time has come, we can hear the turtledove cooing already, there at home. Rouse thee, and come, so beautiful, so well beloved, still hiding thyself as a dove hides in cleft rock or crannied wall."

"It is love alone that counts," said Thérèse to her sister. And as the night began, her agony became more intense than ever, but, "Yes, my God, I *will* everything," she whispered over and over. She wanted to be left for the night, but the Prioress would not allow it, and Sister Marie of the Sacred Heart joined Sister Geneviève for the long vigil.

Thérèse had always been sure that the weather would be fine when she died, but when the first gray streaks of dawn announced the end of that terrible night, they showed a sky of dark clouds. Rain beat down, pattering on the leaves in the garden, trickling down the panes of the infirmary window.

In the gray light that filtered through the rain tracks on the window, the still figure in the bed could now be seen faintly. The bell was ringing for Mass. Sister Marie and Sister Geneviève rose from their chairs by the bed as one of the three doors to the room opened softly and the brown figure of Mother Agnes appeared. She was to take their place during Mass, and the three spoke a few words about the patient.

For a few moments they were four sisters alone together, Marie, Pauline, Céline, and the youngest, Thérèse, whose silent agony they shared.

Mother Agnes took her place by the bed where her little Thérèse lay, breathing noisily and painfully. Sometimes she opened her eyes for a moment and looked beseechingly at the statue of the Mother of Jesus that stood facing her bed. Once the feeble little hands groped toward each other as they lay on the sheet and the fingers knotted together as if in prayer. "I've prayed so hard to her," came the hoarse whisper, "but it's all nothing but agony, no consolation at all."

All morning it went on. Her strength seemed quite spent, yet to her Sisters' surprise she managed to sit up in bed. Perhaps she would not die yet after all. "Perhaps it will go on for months. I don't believe it's death yet, only more suffering for me, and tomorrow it will be worse!" But she would not give in. "So much the better!" she cried defiantly.

As the morning passed and the rain drummed on the windows, she hardly spoke but lay shifting and restless in her pain, gasping for breath and muttering feebly. Sometimes a few words broke through and were spoken aloud, driven from her by some new horror of pain. "Oh my God! I love him—he is good. Sweet Holy Virgin, come and help me!" And suddenly a cry of real fear: "If this is the agony, then what will death be like?"

When the Prioress came to see her, she struggled to speak to her. "Mother, I assure you the cup is full today. But God won't abandon me—he has never abandoned me!" Later she begged them to pray for her, and as some fresh pain seemed to attack her, she cried in the teeth of it, "My God, my God, you are so good! I know it!"

At three o'clock she stretched out her arms like Christ on the Cross as she lay propped against the high pillow. On one side knelt Mother Agnes, watching with agonized tenderness the child she had brought up. The Prioress's stern face was gentle now as she, too, watched the suffering of her much-loved and much-scolded daughter. She put a little picture of Our Lady of Mount Carmel on Thérèse's knees. Thérèse looked down at it for a moment and then turned her head a little to look at Mother Marie anxiously. "Oh, Mother, present me to the Blessed Virgin—get me ready to die well."

"You have always understood and practiced humility," Mother Marie reassured her, "so you have made your preparation for death already."

The strained face on the pillow relaxed. "Yes," she said peacefully, "I think I've never wanted anything but the truth—yes, I have understood humility of heart."

Through the afternoon the Sisters watched beside her by turns or together. Sometimes it seemed to them that she was like the martyrs, upheld by God's power when human strength would have failed. As if to reassure them, "I am not sorry to have given myself up to love," she said again and again. "Oh, no. I am not sorry—quite the opposite."

Wondering, they listened to the words she spoke half to herself. "I would never have believed it possible to suffer so much," she whispered, "never, never! I can only explain it by my burning desire to save souls. I can't breathe—I can't die." But she was not conquered. "I'm quite willing to suffer more!" Later she said, "I have been granted all my smallest wishes. So the greatest of them must be granted, too—to die of love!"

At half-past four, Mother Agnes was watching alone, when suddenly she noticed a change in the gray face on the pillow and rang the infirmary bell to call the community.

From all over the convent the nuns came, leaving their work, to kneel by their Sister and help her in her last battle. As they came into the room, Thérèse turned her head on the pillow and smiled at each one, then she turned back to the crucifix that was clutched between her knotted fingers. Every breath made her give little cries. Sister Geneviève leaned over and touched her dry, cracked lips with a piece of ice, and looking up, Thérèse managed a last smile for Céline.

As she knelt by the bed, Mother Agnes heard the sound of twittering. Turning for a moment, she saw through the wide-open window a crowd of little birds singing and singing as they prepared for their flight to a warmer country. They seemed heartless, she thought, singing so gaily out there, when inside this child of hers lay dying.

For two hours it went on. When the Angelus sounded at six, Thérèse opened her eyes and looked up at the statue of Mary, Mother of Jesus. The Gospel of Luke tells how God's messenger brought to a peasant girl in Nazareth the news of her tremendous and terrifying calling. And her reply has come down to us in the words that are part of the ancient prayer of the Angelus: "Behold the handmaid of the Lord, let it be done to me as you have said." Her reply was Thérèse's reply to everything that God asked of her.

A little after seven the Prioress sent the community away, for it seemed as if Thérèse might live for some hours yet. Pitifully, Thérèse turned to her. "Mother, isn't this the agony yet? Am I not going to die yet?"

"Yes, child, it is the agony—but perhaps God wishes it to go on for a few hours still."

It was a hard thing to have to say, but Thérèse seemed once more to gather up all her courage. "Very well," she said, "so be it—oh, I don't want to suffer less." She turned to her crucifix and looked at it for a long moment. At last her voice was heard once more, in a whisper that summed up her whole life. "Oh, I love him—my God—I—love—you!"

Then she fell back against the pillows, and her head leaned a little to the right like the head of the crucified figure that she held in her hands.

The watching Sisters thought she was dead, and the Prioress turned to one of them. "Ring the bell quickly," she said, and once more the loud clanging sounded all over the convent. "Open all the doors!" ordered Mother Marie, and to the three who heard her it seemed that in Heaven also those words must sound, where the Lord gave his command to the angels at the gates of the Holy City, saying, "Open all the doors!"

Swiftly, with a rustling of habits and shuffling of rope soles, the nuns gathered and knelt around the bed. They saw that the face on the pillow was no longer flushed but pale and glowing like a lily.

Thérèse opened her eyes, but she did not seem to see the drab curtains of her bed, the statue at the foot, the walls of the infirmary. Sister Marie of the Eucharist rose softly, and taking the lighted candle from the table, she held it before her cousin's eyes. But their gaze did not flicker, and the watchers knew that for Sister Thérèse the gates of Heaven were opening at last. Once or twice she moved her head on the pillow, then with a little sigh she closed her eyes, and they saw that she was dead. It was twenty minutes past seven, September 30, 1897.

For a time there was no sound in the room. Then in the silence they realized that the noise of the rain had stopped, and when they looked toward the window, they saw that the stars shone brilliantly in a clear sky.

Slowly the nuns left the room, leaving only Mother Agnes and Sister Marie of the Sacred Heart, who, with the old infirmarian, were to lay out the body for burial. As they washed the body of the twenty-four-year-old nun and dressed her in a clean habit, they told each other with tears how very young and frail she looked. "You wouldn't think she was more than twelve or thirteen," said Mother Agnes.

And still she seemed to smile with heavenly happiness. They put a crown of white roses on her head and a palm branch in her hand. They laid her on the straw mattress from her cell, and all the nuns came to pay a last visit to their Sister. Seeing her so radiantly beautiful, they went away with peace and joy. Then she was laid in the choir near the grille of the public chapel.

The crowds who came to see her found again the "little queen" of the old days, for her uncovered face was full of serene dignity.

Four days afterward she was buried in the corner of the public cemetery that was kept for the Carmelites. Some days later a wooden cross was put up over her grave, and a few people who came there out of affection or curiosity saw on it some words that they could not understand.

"Je veux passer mon Ciel à faire du bien sur la terre," it said. "I want to spend my Heaven in doing good on earth."

$\mathcal{P}ostscript$

W HEN A CARMELITE dies, her convent usually sends a short account of her life to other Carmels, as Mother Agnes had mentioned to the Prioress when she wanted Thérèse to finish the story of her life. And after Thérèse was dead, the two stories were indeed used to form the obituary circular, together with her "letter" to Sister Marie of the Sacred Heart. But first it was considerably altered. For one thing, Mother Marie Gonzaga wanted it to appear that the whole thing had been written for *her,* instead of only the second part of the story. For another, there were many passages that Mother Agnes considered too intimate or too ordinary or not sufficiently "edifying" for publication. And the book was added to, to make it seem as saintly as possible, for Thérèse's sisters were convinced that she was indeed a saint. It was all done with the best possible intentions, and the same intentions guided a monk called Dom Madeleine, who was consulted about it and who made further vigorous cuts and additions. He also gave the book its title, *The Story of a Soul.* Then the result was submitted to the Bishop for permission to publish, and he gave it.

The book that was published was therefore very different from what Thérèse had originally written. Everything that was even mildly critical of anyone in Carmel had been cut out, as well as all the funny childhood incidents that were not considered becoming to a saint. Many passages had been toned down and made more conventionally pious. But even so, the nuns were taking a risk, and the fact that the publication went ahead at all shows how impressed they were with Thérèse's sanctity. When the stacks of books arrived from the printers, some of the nuns said in dismay, "What shall we do with all these? We shall have them all left on our hands!"

Copies were sent to the other convents, and it soon became apparent that even in its altered and sweetened form, Thérèse's message was spiritual dynamite. One or two Carmelite convents were so shocked by her daring approach to God, her conviction that love was enough, that they refused to have the book in their convents. But others read it and, moved and startled, lent it to relations and friends outside their convents. Soon a trickle of letters began to arrive at the Lisieux Carmel, asking for more copies. Gradually, the trickle increased to a stream, and the stream to a flood. The first printing was soon exhausted; it was reprinted and then again reprinted, and still the demand grew. Edition after edition appeared. Within seven years *The Story of a Soul* had been translated into English, Polish, Dutch, Italian, and Portuguese.

Thérèse's fame increased steadily, and soon Catholics began to realize that she was truly a messenger from God to the modern world. In the end the gratitude of those Thérèse had helped, and the hope and faith she inspired, were publicly expressed when the Pope declared that Thérèse Martin was a Saint. The gorgeous ceremony of canonization took place in St. Peter's in Rome, on May 19, 1925. But this public acclamation was only expressing what millions of ordinary people had known for years—that Thérèse Martin could help them to find God in their everyday lives.

Hundreds of books have been written about Thérèse Martin, and still more appear every year. About twelve years ago, after the death of Mother Agnes, original manuscripts of Thérèse's writings became available, as well as her letters. For the first time, people could read exactly what she had written, without cuts or alterations. The fact that it took so long for the manuscripts to be "allowed out" shows very clearly how extraordinarily new and strange Thérèse's ideas seemed to the people among whom she lived. Now we find them less surprising, but the strength and freshness of her writing is still as impressive as when she first wrote. What is so special about Thérèse? Why are there so many books about her? Why do so many people find her ideas an inspiration—people who are not nuns, often not even Catholics?

One reason is that Thérèse is so near. There are photographs and snapshots of her—snapshots of a saint. It is startling, if one is used to thinking of a saint as someone in a stained-glass window draped in medieval robes. When her manuscripts were first released, they were published in a facsimile edition—each page was photographed, printed on pages exactly the size, shape, and color of the pages of the exercise books she wrote in, and bound in exactly the same kind of cover as the actual ones in which she wrote. So it is possible to see and handle and read her tiny, strong writing, filling the pages of a schoolgirl's cheap exercise book. It is an odd experience and brings her very close. One can almost feel that Thérèse has that moment laid down her pen, to rest a little. She is so ordinary, so like other people. If she were still alive, she would be a very old lady—but there are old ladies living who were born before Thérèse. This is a saint who lives next door to all of us.

That is part of the reason. And the other, bigger reason is linked to this. Thérèse brings into the ordinary, modern world the sort of violent, uncompromising love that Christ has always inspired in people who discovered him, ever since he walked on the roads of Palestine. But so often, we can see him only through the minds of people who thought in ways that are quite different from the way we think. So we get the idea that the following of Christ is something that belongs to strange, archaic language and thought, strange martyrdoms, and a solemn religious atmosphere. People read the Gospels and admire the saints and say, "This isn't for me. What has all this to do with my life?"

What Thérèse did was to show that a heroic love—heroic, sometimes, to the point of madness—can be worked out in the ordinary details of a life that is, in most people's eyes, utterly dull and pointless.

Thérèse was a nun, an enclosed, contemplative nun. With her kind of upbringing, that was the most likely way for her to choose to respond to the demands of love. But the call to love comes to everyone, and it makes no difference whether one is married or single, clever or simple, old or young—all that is necessary is to say "yes," as Thérèse did. Every day, even every hour, the opportunities come. To be kind to someone or to snub them, to finish a dull bit of work or to find an excuse to leave it, to spend time on someone else's needs or to get in a corner with a book—the list could go on for pages and never be complete. To all the tiny opportunities, Thérèse gave the answer of love. That is all that is necessary, she tells us. Faults and quirks of character don't matter. Only love. And nothing else is any good, because "good" actions that aren't loving don't bring us to God.

The tiny things are not really so tiny, because they are

done for love, and a person who says "yes" to the little demands of love will end by saying "yes" to the huge and even extraordinary demands, too. It seems so easy, in imagination, to be a hero or heroine in dramatic and dangerous circumstances. Thérèse shows that heroism over the big things grows only from heroism over little things—unnoticed, unexciting heroism that is real because it is loving.

This account of Thérèse's short life is written for people who are about the same age as she was when she decided to be a Carmelite. It is not very long; therefore, I have left out a lot that is interesting and important. But everything in the book is authentic—nothing is made up. I hope that other people who are thinking about growing up and about what life is all about will find it a help to see how Thérèse tackled these problems and made mistakes and pushed ahead and hammered out an understanding of life that has already been an inspiration to millions. If the portrait of Thérèse that this book presents seems attractive, I hope that those who read it will go on to read her own autobiography and her letters.

But Thérèse would not be pleased to think that people who read about her stopped at liking and admiring her. Her whole life and all that she wrote had one purpose: to help others to know the love that filled her. She wanted people to know the source of that love, of all love: the life of God that comes to us in the man Jesus Christ. So the best response to her life and her teaching is to realize where it came from, to think it over, and to pray. Then, when we meet Christ somewhere or other (he turns up in all sorts of places, not just in Carmelite convents), we shall recognize him and say "yes" to all that he asks.

Grasping Things

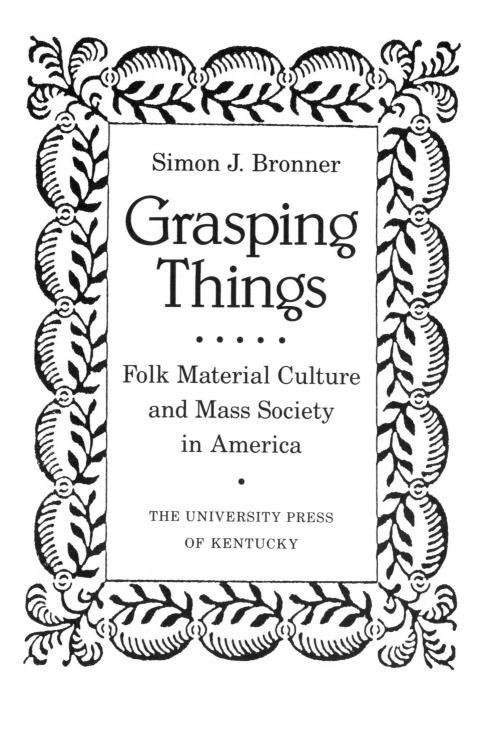

Simon J. Bronner

Grasping
Things

· · · · · ·

Folk Material Culture
and Mass Society
in America

·

THE UNIVERSITY PRESS
OF KENTUCKY

Scholarly publisher for the Commonwealth,
serving Bellarmine College, Berea College, Centre
College of Kentucky, Eastern Kentucky University,
The Filson Club, Georgetown College, Kentucky
Historical Society, Kentucky State University,
Morehead State University, Murray State University,
Northern Kentucky University, Transylvania University,
University of Kentucky, University of Louisville,
and Western Kentucky University.

Editorial and Sales Offices: Lexington, Kentucky 40506-0024

Library of Congress Cataloging-in-Publication Data

Bronner, Simon J.
 Grasping things.

 Bibliography: p.
 Includes index.
 1. Material culture—United States.
2. United States—Social life and customs. 3. Dwellings
—United States. 4. Folk art—United States. 5. Food
habits—United States. 6. Material culture—
Pennsylvania. 7. Material culture—Indiana.
8. Pennsylvania—Social life and customs. 9. Indiana—
Social life and customs. I. Title.
E161.B78 1986   306'.0973   85-22473
ISBN 0-8131-1572-8